"I've known Cody for years. His resilience and purpose following an injury that was so devastating, no one gave him a chance of survival. Like Cody, I was burned beyond recognition in Vietnam and had to return from the brink of death. His story is compelling and inspiring. I relate to his amazing parallel of physical scars that mimic the spiritual and emotional scars that restrict our progress toward recovery. A must read, to say the least."

—Dr. Dave Roever
President and CEO
OPERATION WARRIOR RECONNECT
US Navy Special Warfare Command. Vietnam

"I can't stop raving about Scar Release to family, friends, and colleagues. From trails to triumphs, from a victim to survivor, from despair to hope, Cody shares his story in an enlightening, empowering and engaging manner that will invoke change and courage in any reader. Everyone should take the time to read this book."

—Dustin K. Wise, MBA., MHCL,
Author of *Don't Allow Your Scars to Determine Your Destiny*
President and CEO, The Wise Foundation
Chief Operating Officer, Preferred Pediatric Health Care

"In this book, Cody teaches us that our scars are NOT meant to be shamefully hidden in the shadows. They are divine reminders of what we have powerfully survived. Cody's recovery is certainly proof that miracles do exist. However, the greatest miracle (in my opinion) is the global transformation Cody has chosen to inspire with his scars."

—Dr. Sean C. Stephenson
Professional Speaker, Therapist,
and Author of *Get Off Your But*

———————

"When Cody Byrns' world was rocked by a fiery crash that left him with devastating burn injuries over 37% of his body, he began the fight of his life. His story of miraculous recovery through hard work, the support of his faith, loving family, and medical team will inspire the reader to say, "I 2 CAN Overcome!" A must-read proving that "Attitude really is everything!" You will be inspired!"

—Ruth Brubaker Rimmer, PhD, CLCP
Burn Psychologist/Researcher

"Cody's testimony is like none other. His life-changing story is one of courage and commitment."

—Matt Roever
Vice President of the Roever Foundation

"Burns are a forever problem. The individual who has sustained a burn must show patience, true grit, and faith in order to not only survive, but to thrive. Cody Byrns demonstrated all of these qualities and so much more."

—Rajiv Sood, M.D., F.A.C.S.
Chief of Plastic Surgery & Medical Director at
The Richard M. Fairbanks Burn Center in Indianapolis, IN

Thank You, Allison!

SCAR RELEASE

BREAKING FREE OF YESTERDAY'S TROUBLES

CODY BYRNS

Scar Release: Breaking Free of Yesterday's Troubles

Published by

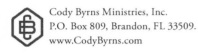

Cody Byrns Ministries, Inc.
P.O. Box 809, Brandon, FL 33509.
www.CodyByrns.com

Printed in the United States of America

First Edition

ISBN-10: 0692045252
ISBN-13: 978-0692045251

This book is dedicated to my family: Allen, Jan, Shane, Jesse, and Toby, who have been there with me every step of the way, along with everyone who has prayed, supported, and encouraged me during my recovery. I would also like to show my appreciation to the Gibson County Fire Department and all of the first responders who took part in rescuing me on May 31, 2013. Also, a big thank you to Dr. Sood and the entire team at The Richard M. Fairbanks Burn Center in Indianapolis, IN as well as everyone who has assisted me in my daily therapy.

TABLE OF CONTENTS

PREFACE

If you have picked up this book because something bad has happened in your life, or if you are facing a great difficulty and don't already have a strong faith in God, I'm going to ask you to consider me an example of how God loves us and works in our lives to bring about good, even, sometimes, in the face of great human tragedy. I was in a horrific car crash in May of 2013. It left me with third- and fourth-degree burns over much of my body, and it devastated my physical and emotional well-being.

I have come through my initial ordeal and I am dealing with it on a continuing, daily basis in a positive, life-affirming way (most days, anyway). I will tell you how I have been able to do this.

I came into this mess with a lifelong strong faith in God. For as long as I can remember, I have loved God and wanted to help spread His Word. However, even though I, to this day, feel blessed, I have had questions about why God allowed this to happen to me. Some days were very difficult.

So, if you don't know much about God, bear with me,

and take the description of my struggles with Him as an introduction to what true love is. Take it as a guide to start you on your own journey to finding your answers. Take it as hope. Don't brush my story off by saying you just don't believe in what I do. Start the journey and see what happens.

Throughout the book, I will tell you what I believe about God, heaven, hell, free will, Jesus Christ, and why bad things happen in our world. While I believe there is a core *love and discipline* in God's guidance to us, this book's purpose is not to dissect everything in the Bible. I believe that the depth of our understanding of the Bible will change and grow as we, ourselves, change and grow.

If you already have a strong faith in God, I hope this book emboldens you to go and live further in God.

INTRODUCTION

In May of 2013 I was young, strong, and healthy. I had just turned twenty-three years old. Despite my age, I was extremely purpose-driven and strove daily to pursue the calling God had placed on my life. My ultimate goal was to travel the world and inspire people as a children's pastor and traveling evangelist and entertainer. But one day, in a matter of moments, I nearly lost all of it.

■ ■ ■

The morning of Friday, May 31, 2013 was just like any other morning. My alarm woke me up, I jumped into the shower, grabbed some breakfast, and drove to church to start my workday. On Fridays, I was in persistent study mode for the upcoming Sunday service. During lunch that day, I was scheduled for a meeting to discuss an upcoming juggling and comedy performance for the following weekend at the Red Skelton Performing Arts Center in Vincennes, Indiana.

The meeting went well. Everyone was excited about the upcoming performance. While trying to contain my excitement, I drove back to my church office to finish up the rest of the day. On the way back to my office, I found myself stopped at a red light. While stopped, I was rear-ended by a large box truck traveling at full highway speed (60–65 mph). My car was engulfed in flames.

I don't remember anything after the collision. I can tell you that it was bad, and I could have been killed. Yet instead of my life coming to an end that day, I like to think that it was when it all began.

As a result of that fiery crash, my body was covered in third- and fourth-degree burns. I have permanent scars on almost forty percent of my body. My lifestyle has changed completely. The car crash didn't just scar me physically; I also received multiple internal scars that have had a lasting impact on my emotions and thoughts. It's easy to focus on healing the external wound, but it was the internal scars that made my recovery so challenging.

Working to heal, both internally and externally, from the crash was extremely difficult. But after much prayer, therapy, and study, I discovered the steps needed to find freedom from yesterday's troubles. I now have the freedom to be me! I'm a proud Christian who actively participates in motivating and encouraging crowds of all ages. I am thankful to be able to assist other burn survivors with my own nonprofit, Burn Foundation. To me, this is just the beginning, as I am continuously seeking and finding ways to better today's world. I fully believe that all of this is possible because I consciously decided to make a choice to not allow my scars to limit me from living a full life.

While we may not all be healing from third- and fourth-degree burn scars, I think it's safe to say that every one of us has dealt with—or is still dealing with—emotional or physical scars, or both. If you are not careful, these scars can keep you limited in many areas of your life. For example, they can make it difficult to fully live with your spouse or family. They can even hinder your business endeavors and goals. My hope is that by reading this book, you will discover a real sense of freedom.

Truly looking at our scars is difficult and scary. When we take the time to examine how we've been hurt, it can bring up long-buried feelings of pain, betrayal, and loss. At first glance, our scars can appear ugly and horrifying. However, as you begin to awaken to this new reality that I'm about to share, these scars can also be beautiful.

Today, I want to challenge you to look within yourself and dive into the study of a surgical procedure. I have gone through this actual surgery with my physical burn scars, but I see a parallel in this procedure to emotional scarring. With this understanding, I hope that these steps I took can encourage you to also be willing to walk through the process in your own life.

1

MEETING CHAOS

June 19, 2013. A soft *beep...beep...beep* stirs me awake, and I hear my mom and dad's voices. I've heard my mom speak all of my life, but I've never heard her sound quite like this before. She's not only concerned—she's terrified. As I slowly begin to register my surroundings, she explains that I'm in Indianapolis, in the burn unit, and that I have been in a horrific car crash.

She states that my car was hit by a refrigerator box truck that didn't stop at a red light. She informs me that though I am severely burned, with broken vertebrae, I'm going to be okay. I try to comprehend all of this while actively trying to shake off the last bits of unconsciousness from my body. I look at my mother and see that she has tears in her eyes.

"Cody, your car exploded into flames. The first responders thought you were dead. They called the coroner and everything; then they saw your hand move. They transported you to the hospital through life flight, but quickly rerouted to this burn unit."

I am overtaken by a sense of urgency.

"But, Mom, I have a show next weekend!"

She replies, "Cody, your burns were so severe that you've been in a medically induced coma and on full life support for three weeks."

I felt as though three weeks of my life had been stolen from me. It's almost impossible to describe the feeling of losing a whole chunk of your life. I was driving, and the next thing I knew, I was in a hospital? Imagine if you were to take a quick, twenty-minute power nap, and then wake up and learn that almost a month has passed since you fell asleep.

Scary, right? So much confusion. So many questions. This is exactly how I felt.

I was heavily medicated at the time, and I wasn't able to fully grasp the gravity of my new reality for a few days. It was much later when I discovered the intensity of how this tragedy affected my family. The doctors had told my family members they couldn't touch me. Even worse: my oxygen levels were very low, and there were a couple of times I came close to dying. After I was out of the coma, my parents told me I was in such bad shape for the first few surgeries that they couldn't move my body into the operating room without inflicting more damage. They had to perform these incredibly dangerous surgeries in my ICU room. These moments were harrowing for my loved ones.

When they were finally able to bring me out of the coma, they said my body shook with such intensity that my hospital bed moved erratically. My body had grown so addicted to the medication that was pumped through my veins that when it left my system the result was uncontrollable tremors. My doctors advised the nurses to gently wean me off the medicine to help me wake up.

Even when I came out of the coma, I still had to remain on life support for a few days. I was on life support for so long, the doctors mentioned putting something called a "trach" in me to assist with my breathing. However, when they saw that I was fighting to survive, they knew I could handle coming off life support and breathe on my own.

But waking from the coma and coming off life support were only the first steps of this very long journey. I was frightened for my well-being, and worried about what the days ahead would look like as I began to heal. My room was frequently filled with doctors and nurses, who scanned my body up and down with their eyes. Modesty went out the window, as my body lay completely vulnerable to everyone. The doctors and nurses were constantly talking among themselves about me, as if I wasn't there. Pictures were also always being taken. I felt a bit like a lab rat, as they monitored the healing stages.

One doctor even began giving orders as to what needed to take place. In the midst of this commotion, I had no idea what he was talking about. At that point, I was wearing a neck brace due to my back being broken, and I could not sit up in my bed. I could not see my lower body. When I heard the doctors and nurses talk about me, my worst fears ran wild. I didn't know what they were seeing on my body that I couldn't. I was filled with dread over how I looked. I was heartbroken, and couldn't believe this was happening to me.

As I tried to calm myself, tears streamed down my face. My life as I had known it was over. Nothing would ever be the same, and I knew it. When the doctors left, and the days continued, I found myself trapped in my own thoughts:

> *All I ever wanted to do in this life was to help make other people happy. All of my dreams are shattered now. This pain I'm feeling is like a*

bed of knives ripping through every layer of my flesh. I'm being skinned alive as they harvest what skin I have left to cover these holes in my body. My muscles and bones ache so bad. I am just longing to be put to sleep in the hope that it will be gone when I wake up. I look like a mummy, wrapped in these bandages. It's hot as hell in this room. I'm incredibly thirsty but unable to drink liquids, only gelled water. What is silent aspiration? Because they keep saying I have it. These bandages are completely soaked with blood and fluid. I am scared to see what I look like. The stench is unbearable. This is getting old, fast.

Lying here, so dirty and exposed, I have never been so embarrassed. These nurses come in here day in and day out, washing my private parts. I'm constipated to the point of screaming, and yet I am so afraid of my bladder filling because I hate being catheterized. How will people look at me beyond these walls? How will I function in life? How am I going to live with these scars?

I had never thought it would happen to me, but I was struck by tragedy, awakened by this unexpected chaos. I'd worked in ministry, helping people learn about Jesus. A devastating accident like this could never happen to me. And yet, there I was, lying in a hospital bed, trusting medical professionals to heal my broken body.

My injuries were severe. I had two broken vertebrae and many torn ligaments. I fought blood infections and lumps in my body called hematomas. But for me, the most tragic part of these injuries was the fact that I was afflicted with third- and fourth-degree burns. I'd never in my life heard of a fourth-degree burn.

My burn injuries required careful attention, especially as my body was trying to heal. The healing process, after receiving skin grafts, consists of the body producing scar tissue, which I was well aware of. I knew I would carry the marks of this car crash for the rest of my life. Things would never go back to the way they had been. Learning to accept this was easier said than done.

Questions for Reflection

Through this chapter, we discover how chaos comes unexpectedly.

Have you ever encountered an unexpected tragedy?

If so, how did it make you feel? Were you frightened?

How have these experiences affected you in your daily living?

Do you find yourself permanently marked (scarred) by these traumatic events?

*Be sure to sign up at **www.ScarReleaseBook.com** to receive a **FREE study guide** to assist you in walking through your scar-release journey.*

2

UNDERSTANDING THE SCAR

Days and weeks went by as doctors and nurses monitored my healing process. I was still trying to understand that my body was now disfigured. I would never look like I once had. Coming to terms with this was nothing short of mortifying. These new markings were now a part of me—forever! But beyond their physical appearance, I soon learned that these scars would require me to live differently. They would hinder my ability to move in the way I used to. I was suddenly carrying a load of turmoil I hadn't asked for.

Have you ever felt this way? Have you ever found yourself awakened to a new reality that has left you with an indelible mark?

What is a scar, exactly? According to the *Merriam-Webster's Medical Dictionary*, a scar is: "A mark left (as in the skin) by the healing of injured tissue," or, "A lasting emotional injury."[1]

I now have numerous large, physical, permanent scars on my body. But this wreck created more than just physical scarring; it created emotional scarring as well. I believe any trauma that takes place in our lives can cause psychological hurdles that we eventually need to face and overcome. It can make us feel helpless when we try to face them, because these problems seem bigger than we are. These emotional scars can be seen in our everyday behaviors and actions, and can often affect those around us. These scars are probably the hardest to heal.

Many people suffer from emotional scars. Just like a physical scar, an emotional one can come in many forms. Scars are traumatizing, especially when we look back at the event that caused them and their side effects. I remember the trauma of waking up to a devastating nightmare. The first time I caught a glimpse of the scarring on my body, I felt as though a part of me had died. But it was necessary for me to see the scars, in order to move on and become independent again. It was incredibly challenging, on many levels.

I was in the burn unit for a total of two-and-a-half months. When I left, I was transported by ambulance to a rehabilitation hospital. I had to relearn everything, even how to walk. It was so hard to wrap my mind around the idea that I could no longer do something as effortless as walking; I felt like I was restarting my life from square one.

A few weeks after I came out of the coma, and while I was still in the burn unit, annoyance was starting to set in. I grew extremely tired of being catheterized. I genuinely believed that if I could only get up, out of the bed, and walk to the toilet, I'd be able to pee on my own, without any help.

Have you ever tried to pee while lying in bed? Well, don't try it. But, in my case, the nurses encouraged it. As the nurses tried to encourage me to pee in the urine bottle while I was lying down, I kept insisting that I could walk to the restroom. The nurses kindly told me I couldn't walk. I was bound and determined to prove them wrong.

Once they saw my determination, they called on a physical therapist to join me in the room, to assist me in getting up. As I moved toward the edge of the bed, I cried out in agony. It was the most unbearable pain I have ever felt. I wouldn't wish this pain on my worst enemy.

As I began to fight through the pain, the therapists grabbed my arms and tried to assist me in standing up. As I tried to stand, I realized my weakness, and quickly knew that there was no way I'd be walking to the restroom on my own. The pain was too much, and I couldn't make the short journey, even with help. This revelation took a toll on my mind. I couldn't believe it!

It was slowly dawning on me that my road to recovery was going to be much longer than I'd realized. The process of getting from Point A to Point B wasn't going to be instantaneous; rather, it would require time and patience.

After I was released from the burn unit, I spent a total of six weeks in an inpatient rehabilitation hospital, where doctors and nurses monitored me 24/7. Once I became stable enough to walk and move on my own, I was approved by doctors to leave the facility for a short time. On my release day, I stepped outside the facility, attempting to get into my parents' vehicle while wearing splints, bandages, and a full upper-body brace. Walking stiffly, I felt like Frankenstein. Up to this point I hadn't been in a vehicle that wasn't an ambulance of some sort, but I longed to visit my hometown of Princeton, Indiana for a few days.

The physical therapist was assisting me at the time, but I was heartbroken when I realized I couldn't sit down in the SUV. The reason was that my left leg was burned so badly it had caused a massive buildup of scarring. My range of motion was extremely limited, so I couldn't bend my knee in order to sit. My daily therapy had to continue before I could leave for home.

I was frustrated. All I had wanted to do was spend some time at home, but I couldn't even get my body to sit in a car. After a few days of therapy, the therapist discovered a clever way for me to sit without the need to bend my left leg. Finally, I got to visit my hometown. Unfortunately, I couldn't stay long because I had outpatient therapy to complete in Indianapolis.

Before getting too far ahead of myself, I want to explain more about the critical recovery stages I went through in rehab.

Burn injuries are extremely painful, from start to finish—receiving them, and recovering from them. But fear is also a large part of recovering from burns—fear of the unknown. I had no idea what my body looked like, because of my neck brace and bandages. I was scared to think about what I looked like. I wondered if I would ever do the things I loved again.

I was able to catch a glimpse of my body when the nurses were redressing my wounds. If you've never experienced redressing a severe burn, trust me when I say that it is a miserable process. Thank God I was still heavily medicated, because it was unbelievably painful. Once in the morning and once at night, the nurses would come in and spend about four to six hours changing my bandages.

It was unpleasant, it was lengthy, and it was heart-breaking, but it was necessary. Doing the work of removing the old, soiled bandages, and inspecting and cleaning the wounds, was a critical part of my body's healing. It's how you treat any deep wound, cleaning the affected area and redressing the wound so it can heal. The only way we can ever heal is if we know exactly what the wound looks like, and then take the steps to aid its healing.

It was horrifying for me to see my body for the first time after the accident. I waited four months to get a good look at myself. As I first looked, I saw the missing parts of my body. Layers of skin had melted or been cut away. That moment was when it really hit me: I had been burnt down to the muscle and bone.

The bone of my left kneecap was exposed, black, and charred. My left side had big indentations from skin and fat being removed. It was almost as if an ice-cream scoop had gone through and scooped it all away. I looked like a creature from a horror film.

Although I didn't have any limbs amputated (fourth-degree burns usually result in amputation), I still couldn't believe that the man in the mirror was me. I was crushed and moved to tears. My heart was broken when I saw the effects of the flames. I had never wept so hard in my life.

For a long time, it was difficult for me to even look at myself, but I had no choice. Every time I took a bath, I had to look at the scars and acknowledge them. Even though it was hard, I had to suck up the pain.

For the first few months, the water touching my skin would often result in screams of agony. I was dealing with so much discomfort, every touch from a nurse, every movement of the dressing changes, was a living nightmare. When looking at myself, I saw every aspect of my life's plans crumble before my eyes. Juggling, traveling, speaking—even my friendships were affected.

These new markings caused me to ponder how I would be viewed beyond the hospital walls. Would I be seen as a monster? Would I get awkward stares from people in public? The kids I'd once had the privilege of teaching at church—how would they see me? As a young man who wasn't married, would I ever find someone to love me? Would I ever fall in love? How would my future kids see their daddy? As my burns healed into scars, I felt this new life being engraved into me.

Isn't it interesting that just looking at a scar is painful and hard to comprehend? Tears can flow when we catch a glimpse of the scars we carry for the first time.

My doctors explained to me that burn scars (also known

as contracture scars) appear after receiving a skin graft. They may heal outwardly, but the scar can grow deeper and heal in a way that causes tightening in the skin and creates immobility, especially if the skin heals and grows around a joint or ligament. Many burn survivors have encountered this problem, leaving us with limited joint mobility. The solution to freeing the scar is called a "surgical contracture release" or "scar release." According to *Achauer and Sood's Burn Surgery Reconstruction and Rehabilitation*, by Dr. Rajiv Sood, "Surgical intervention is necessary if conservative therapy treatments are unsuccessful. The most common areas that require surgical release are the anterior neck, elbows, and shoulders."[2]

Surgical intervention was definitely in order for my right wrist and the web space between my fingers, as well as my right foot and left knee. These joints weren't regaining flexibility, despite intense therapy. As a juggler, not having the use of my fingers and hands was a pretty huge deal. My performance was hindered, and my web spaces were becoming so contracted that I couldn't hold on to a water bottle. I needed more than just therapy; I needed surgery. While attending multiple therapy sessions and doctors' appointments, I kept hearing the term "scar release." The more I thought about what needed to be done during this process, medically speaking, the more I thought that this was exactly what I needed.

As I came to understand the procedure, I started to see a parallel. My physical scars restricted me, which, in turn, limited my ability to do things. Just as we can physically be affected by immobility, we can also become emotionally immobile. When this happens, we can find ourselves stuck.

Have you ever found yourself stuck? It's a horrible experience. I believe that many people have been troubled by something to the point that it has scarred them. While a scar doesn't have to be a bad thing, a scar does become a bad thing when it limits your ability to live a positive life.

I suffered inward scarring because of this experience. It affected my normal way of thinking, manifesting as PTSD (post-traumatic stress disorder), for quite some time. I was anxious, I was on edge, and it would take seemingly innocuous things to trigger my PTSD. A loud noise, a dog barking, or a siren sounding somewhere within earshot could send me reeling. I was certainly hurting physically, but I began to notice that I had been severely injured on an emotional level as well.

Without warning, my insecurity started to express itself. When I looked in the mirror, I would have disturbing flashbacks. They would hit me from nowhere. For years I had battled with being overweight. But ultimately, fat can be removed from a person's body; scars cannot. My self-worth seemed to diminish right before my eyes. Once again, I battled with the fear of how people would look at me or treat me as.

Would I have a new identity? Would I be known as "Cody Byrns, the man who is now burned and scarred?" I saw the statement clearly, as if it were blown up on a billboard. I mean, it was ironic enough that my last name is pronounced "burns." Would I ever be looked at again as a normal human being, with an intellect and emotions? How would this affect me as a speaker and entertainer who makes people laugh? Would audiences go from laughing with me to laughing at me? Would my appearance be the cover by which people judge me as a person? Then there were those times when I would wonder, "Am I going to be seen as someone who looks so different that I will be pitied?"

I needed to have my independence back. I wasn't walking in freedom. And when I say freedom, I mean not being bound to living in fear and worrying what other people may think of me. My daily activities were being hindered; my soul was being hindered. I was more concerned with the opinions of others than living my life to the fullest! Living life to the fullest looks different for everyone, but I know I wasn't living to my full capacity. I was walking in circles, trying to prove my self-worth.

Questions for Reflection

Were your scars hard to grasp when you first noticed them?

Do you find that your scarring moments have taken away your ability to walk toward your goals in life?

Are you afraid that your scars will destroy your identity?

Do you need a scar release?

*Be sure to sign up at **www.ScarReleaseBook.com** to receive a **FREE study guide** to assist you in walking through your scar-release journey.*

3

WRESTLING WITH FAITH

Freedom is essential to everyone. Allow me to give you the tools that can bring fulfillment when we are in the midst of darkness.

One of the most beneficial tools that helped me through this tragedy has been my faith in Jesus Christ. During this devastation, if I'm honest with you, I was left with questions and puzzled by my injuries. Have you ever questioned your reality? You may or may not consider yourself a Christian, but I think it's safe to say that there have been times in your life when you have wondered about a higher power. Am I right? If so, has there been the question of whether this "higher power" loves or hates you?

I've found it vitally important to read the Bible daily. I wanted to read encouraging scriptures to lift me up during adversity. In my moment of distress, people on social media would post things to me and want to help me. Although it was a beautiful thing, and I understood the sentiment, it became overwhelming. It became especially so when some comments would just confuse me. These people were trying to be encouraging, but I would often wonder if they understood what they were saying.

Some people would quote scriptures to me that made no sense in my situation. They would use the Bible out of context to try and make me feel better. The Bible is useful for assisting individuals in their time of pain and discomfort, but if the scripture is told to someone out of context it can cause harm to their faith. For me, not only did it spark confusion, but it luckily also sparked curiosity to go back to the original text.

Their comments caused me to search the Bible a little deeper. I come from a Christian background, and so I want to analyze some scripture with you. One particular scripture that people frequently quoted to me was Jeremiah 29:11: "'For I know the plans I have for you,'" declares the LORD, "'plans to prosper you and not to harm you, plans to give you hope and a future'" (NIV).

As a Christian, I believe that we are all created for a purpose. I feel that it is extremely important to meet with God daily in prayer to understand our purpose here on earth. I grew up in church, and I knew the common Christian sayings, such as, "God loves you," and, "He will always take care of you." I believe that God loves me and will take care of me. Of course, you might wonder how I can believe that after what I've been through. As I was recovering, I had that question too. I searched through scripture for an answer.

Yes, I was harmed. However, I had to take a step back to understand what God is trying to tell us in this verse from Jeremiah. I am speaking very generally here, but I believe there are a few different reasons God would allow pain in our lives. As we move further along in this book, I will begin to break those ideas down, so it's a little easier to digest.

Jeremiah 29:11 is the perfect example of an incredibly important scripture that is often taken out of context. Have you ever been told a Bible verse that seemed to contradict itself? It's possible that the verse was not recited to you correctly. This happened for me with Jeremiah 29:11. This led me to understand *one* of the reasons God can allow pain and hardship to enter our lives.

This verse was written to the Israelites (God's people), who were in exile at this time, assuring them that He (God) had a plan and that they could trust Him. He sent them into captivity—which is confusing, I know—but God ultimately desired for them to realize their own need for Him. They had to suffer in a place where they didn't want to go in order for God to do *His* work. They were hoping for instant freedom, but God had a different plan. They were to remain in captivity for many more years—seventy, to be exact. His plan wasn't the instant deliverance they were hoping for. They had a hard road that would ultimately lead them to an overabundance of joy.

As we can see, God knew what He was doing, and *allowed* a terrible situation to strengthen His people. One of the reasons they were sent into exile, as we see in Jeremiah, was because they were in a state of disobedience. Their time in captivity gave them the opportunity to learn the importance of being obedient and depending on God.

You could think, "This is really evil," and wonder how God could be looking out for His people's best interests when He sent them into exile. But let me pose this to you: while it may seem like God was doing the Israelites harm, they could only see a portion of the picture, right? Could it be true that God saw the bigger picture ahead of time? God had a reason and a purpose for sending the Israelites into exile. Even though His people were walking into something awful, God was still in control, still working all things together for good.

Picture a parent and a child. That parent is responsible for assisting the child in his or her development. When the child disobeys the parent's directions, the child receives a disciplinary punishment. The parent doesn't discipline without reason. Instead, there is a purpose behind the punishment. The child may not like the parent's decision, but the parent knows things that the child doesn't, and is ultimately looking out for the best interests of the child.

This is how I understand God and the Israelites. When the Israelites were in exile, they were there because God was looking out for their best interests and the interests of all mankind. Although it would take time and come about through a process, God reminded them that He does have a plan to prosper, and not harm, them; it just wasn't how they'd imagined.

"God disciplines those that He loves" (Heb. 12:6). This can seem harsh, but let me reassure you that God loves us and wants the best for His children. God isn't out to harm people. Therefore, when we're in the midst of hardship, we must adjust our mindset for God to *use* difficult circumstances to better equip us for what lies ahead. Tragedy can be *used* as a stepping stone that teaches us life lessons. Ultimately, these difficult moments present us with opportunities to grow stronger in our faith.

God wants good things for us. Sometimes what we perceive as good isn't good in God's eyes. Likewise, we also must understand that those bad things we encounter may be hard right now, but they serve an eternal perspective. God is working on a larger story than what is happening in this moment, and so when we encounter trouble or hardship, or are taken out of our comfort zone, we have to remember that God has a purpose for it all.

After all, we enjoy our comfort, but sometimes what we define as comfort really may be harming us in the long run. Some find comfort in doing drugs, and this can result in being addicted to drugs for life. These drugs can be harmful to the human body. They may be illegal; their users can get caught. This would result in the drug user being put in jail or into a rehab center. For the sake of illustration, let's say the individual went to jail, making him or her a prisoner. To the prisoner, this may seem bad, but if the prisoner changes his or her perspective, this individual will begin to see that maybe jail is the best thing at that time. Being placed behind bars can be used as an opportunity to overcome the addiction that was destroying his or her life. This individual must decide how to look at their situation.

Of course, this isn't the only reason someone might encounter pain and hardship in this life. I do not believe my situation was God disciplining me, like the Israelites being sent to exile, or the result of a poor choice on my part, but it was the result of another person's poor choice. These poor choices take place because we live in a fallen creation, which I will explain further as we go along.

I have concluded that God does have a plan for my life, and this I've always known, but that this crash was an unexpected tragedy. Unexpected to me, but not to God. He knows our future, but God also knows how to take the worst of disasters and use them for our good. As I have stood firmly on Romans 8:28: "And we know that all things work together for good to those who love God, to those who are the called according to His purpose" (NKJV).

This verse can be easy to read but difficult to grasp in times of hardship; trust me, I know. People, like me at the time, can often assume that being a child of God is an opportunity to live a life as we see fit and not have to go through hard times. That is probably why a lot of people stop believing in God. They are quoted certain Bible verses out of context that cause them to drift away into a fairytale fantasy or poor theology.

Life as a Christian isn't always glamorous; often it's the opposite. Being a Christian may not be easy, but it's definitely worth it. Life for everyone, Christian or not, can be difficult. There are times when our plans are wrecked and we face unexpected tragedies. Trouble isn't God's plan for our lives, but troublesome times will happen no matter the plan we pursue.

As a Christian, I am learning more about the importance of not trying to convince God what I want, but rather trying to submit to His will for my life. His plan looks different for different people. If you're a doctor, a stay-at-home mom, a lawyer, plumber, or pastor, be the best at your vocation as you can be. It's through our devotion to living daily with God that we understand His will and plan for our lives.

As far as troublesome times are concerned, it all depends on how we let it affect us. I know it's not easy to live out this perspective in our daily lives, but have faith. God is here for us and He gives us others to help us along our way. Do you see the glass half empty or half full? God has a plan for us, in Christ. Everyone's journey is different.

The moment I became a Christian, I was considered to be among God's people, a child of God. I have an inner hope that comes through my relationship with Jesus Christ. I choose to have a positive mindset about my physical afflictions. While dealing with these burn injuries on a daily basis, I had to discover my positive mindset deep within my soul.

Questions for Reflection

Have you ever wrestled with the idea of there being a higher power?

Do you recognize that you have a purpose?

Do you see your life from a glass half-empty or half-full mindset?

*Be sure to sign up at **www.ScarReleaseBook.com** to receive a **FREE study guide** to assist you in walking through your scar-release journey.*

4

RECOGNIZING WHY
IT HAPPENED

Why me? Why did this happen? Why didn't God stop that truck from hitting me?

I found myself pondering these questions. My scars were caused by the fault of someone who failed to stop at a red light! My whole life, all I wanted to do is help make other people happy. I was known for my talents and helping with child development. So why did I have to suffer from the driver's wrongdoing? Why did I have to live with the results of the driver's poor choice? Why me?

"Why me?" is a popular question for many. It's only normal for us to have these questions. My faith in God was tested during this tragedy. To find freedom from *my* scars, I had to discover the answer to the question, "Why did God allow this to happen?" You may not follow the Christian belief system, and that is okay. I've done a lot of discovery in finding *my* "why." I would like to humbly share my perspective with you.

So, why is there evil in this world? Did God do this to me?

Let me offer you an idea I had to learn to swallow: God is Sovereign. During devastating moments, it is so easy to blame God for the trouble we are in or the heartbreak we are facing. But we live in a fallen creation.

However, while the world is fallen, I serve a God who is bigger than that, *who works all things together for good*. It can be hard to remember this in moments of crisis. I know it was hard for me. But it's a truth that we can cling to when things feel out of control. Let me share a story of something that happened to me not long ago.

A while back, I went to Walgreens to get some photos developed. Some of these photos included images of the crash I had been in. The technician who was working began to question me about the images. I explained what had happened and shared bits of my near-death experience. I even shared with this person that I was a Christian who travels and speaks to provide encouragement. He then said, "We never know why God does these things to us."

I quickly responded, "God doesn't do evil."

He quoted Isaiah 45:7, which says, "I form the light, and create darkness: I make peace, and create evil: I the Lord do all these things" (KJV).

This verse caused me to really wonder, *Does God do evil?* After that encounter, I went home with this on my heart, and I investigated this scripture a little deeper. What if he was right? Did God do this to me? Does God make people do harmful things? Interestingly enough, I was able to resolve this question for myself. The study can be quite long and deep, but I will cut to the chase.

To understand this verse (Isaiah 45:7), we need to view it in context. The word "evil" in this verse was originally written in Hebrew, which is the word "rah." It translates as "trouble, disaster, and calamity."[3]

Within this passage *alone*, we see that God does not create evil in the moral sense, but in the sense of disaster or calamity.[4]

It's important to understand that the context of this passage was foretold in a letter from Isaiah, a prophet, to inform the king of Persia, named Cyrus, years later. God wanted Cyrus to know that He honors obedience and punishes disobedience. This prophecy was referencing the Israelites (God's people). Due to their disobedience, they would undergo God's disciplinary punishment. As we learned, God placed them in exile, but God would use Cyrus to eventually bring them out of captivity.

Once again, God is Sovereign. He is present and just. When we disobey Him, there are consequences. It isn't that God loves us any less. It is simply that, with choices, come consequences. For God's children, those consequences only serve to better us in the long run.

Do my actions play into what happens to me?

All of humanity has a choice of whether or not to serve God. Some believe God to be a bossy control freak who wishes to make our lives miserable. However, I don't believe that to be the case.

Yes, God does tell us how we *should* live. Moses delivered the Ten Commandments (Exod. 20:1-17), and Christ left a path to follow through the Beatitudes (Matt. 5:1-12), the parables, and miracle healings. But this isn't God being bossy. This is God telling us that we have the free will to choose how we will live and giving us guidance in the hope that we will follow it.

The more we follow God's guidance, the closer we get to Him. We become heaven-bound, and as C.S. Lewis points out, we begin to catch glimpses of that glorious place of everlasting and abundant joy, even while still here on earth.

If we choose not to follow the *love* and *discipline* spelled out in God's guidance, we separate ourselves from Him. Separation from God results in misery and everlasting hell. But the good news is that God loves us so much that He sent us His Son, Jesus. With Jesus, we have redemption (John 3:16-18). But we must make the choice to turn away from our sinful nature, declare that Jesus is Lord, and believe in His resurrection as well as live out His teachings in our daily lives.

All of my life, I have wanted to please God, but have I always succeeded at this? No. That's where God's grace comes into play. I mess up (making a poor decision by dis-obeying God's teaching), I repent (tell Christ about my shortcomings and seek forgiveness and purity of heart), and I pursue doing better (a bit wiser this time, hopefully, for the lesson learned). My pursuit of doing better is done out of a love for God because He first loved me.

So, what we do or don't do is critically important. I encourage you to become curious about God's guidance. Look into it yourself. In my search for answers I had to reflect on and study the Bible as a whole, especially the life of Jesus. We shouldn't assume we know it (and like it or don't like it) just because we went to Sunday school as a kid or because we hear sermons or debates on TV and radio from time to time.

Once again, do I believe what happened to me on May 31, 2013 is a result of God punishing me for wrongdoing? Of course not. Even if I had died, I would have expected to wake up in the presence of God Almighty. But for now, I am alive on this earth, and as long as I am living in the flesh, I will battle with suffering (physical pain and emotional hurt).

What happened to me occurred because we live in a broken world, brought about by the exercise of our free will. God, except on very rare occasions (i.e., miracles), will not reverse the painful consequences of the exercise of our free will, even when the consequence may fall on someone other than the offender. To do otherwise would, in effect, take away our free will. But I will tell you what God *does* do... He stays with us through those painful consequences. Some may believe I'm a miracle just to be alive, and some may not. But I do know, for sure, that God has stayed with me.

So, the choice is ours. We struggle with the ups and downs of the gift of free will, probably sometimes wishing we didn't have it. Some may think this is a harsh reality, but it is simply how a world based on free will works. Would we really want it to be any different? And besides, I did not create humankind and I didn't write the Bible. As a Christian, I try to live life accordingly and share my faith with others. God is the Creator, and I am part of His creation. The fact that I am alive on this earth is a gift alone. He has a perfect plan; learning to trust Him with that plan is key.

To better understand this viewpoint, we need to go back to the beginning of humanity, to Adam and Eve. It all starts in the Garden of Eden. The problems in this life do not occur because God caused them, but due to choices that took place in the very beginning. Sadly, God gets blamed for many of the things that He didn't do. *God doesn't do bad things, but He does allow for them.*

You may ask why God allows this trouble to occur in our world. Once again, it is because God has granted humankind the right to choose. Christians draw an understanding from the book of Genesis. When God created Adam and Eve, He told them that they could eat from any tree in the Garden of Eden, but not from the tree of knowledge of good and evil. (Genesis 2:4-3:24).

We know how the story goes; they ate from the tree anyway. When Adam and Eve disobeyed God, that was the moment when sin entered the world. Christians know this as "The Fall of Creation." From that moment, everything changed and was corrupt.

Many may wonder why God would put that tree in the garden to begin with? For years, many theologians and philosophers have debated and pondered this very question. I believe it was a warning, a test for Adam and Eve. They had two options: to create their own stability, or to be stabled by God.

As we read the Bible, there is a clear narrative that God wants a relationship with His creation (humans). I can only imagine how God felt when Adam and Eve disobeyed Him. But, as we know and understand, God gave us the right (free will) to choose and make our own decisions.

Someday, I'd love to have children of my own. I can only imagine how I would feel if I gave my son or daughter a warning not to do something and he or she did it anyway; there would have to be a consequence. Some people may question why God didn't just make us perfect beings or automatically force us to do the right thing. Let's think about this for a second. Indulge me, if you will. If I were to force my future son or daughter to do everything right and love me, then ask yourself this: Would this be genuine love? Definitely not.

Where would our relationship be? I wouldn't want to manipulate my kids into loving me. I would want them to come to me because they trusted me. I would want them to love me for me. I think God would like the same from His children. He knows what's best for us.

Sadly, as humans, we make the mistake of not always trusting God. We even get mad at Him when horrible situations arise in our lives. Often, we find ourselves scarred by our poor choices. God wants us to make good choices; it's why we have free will. If we choose to live out our lives consistently making poor choices, there can be repercussions (internal scarring). I believe that not all, but many, internal scars that exist are because of poor choices. It can be a tough process to get over those poor choices, but if you have the right perspective, it can be used for the better. Remember, I wanted to recognize why bad things happen in our world today. As a Christian, I considered this information extremely valuable. But this still left me with unanswered questions.

"Why did God allow me to be burned and scarred? Why didn't He direct my footsteps more carefully?"

I will never forget a phone call I had with a great hero of faith, and now a mentor, Dr. Dave Roever, during which he shared his story with me. When he was in the line of duty, in Vietnam, he encountered a severe tragedy. During the war, he was about to launch a hand grenade. As he was about to toss it, a sniper shot it before he could release it. As a result, it exploded, causing severe burns to his body. He nearly lost his life. In the beginning stages of his recovery, his emotional healing didn't come quickly, but, it did eventually, after he gave himself the time he needed to deal with his injuries. Dave shares that his burns were third-degree and caused scarring on his entire upper body, including his face. With these permanent scars came depression and suicidal thoughts. However, Dave had a breakthrough. It came through the words that a woman shared with him on national television.

Jan Crouch had invited Dave to be interviewed. Jan and her husband Paul Crouch founded the Trinity Broadcasting Network (TBN). During their interview, she asked Dave, "Dave, do you know why God allowed you to be burned and scarred?" His response was given in frustration, "No! I don't." She then made a statement: "Davey, God didn't do this *to* you, but He allowed it to happen because He could trust you with the scars."

Wow! Let's think about this statement for a second. God trusted Dave with such scars. God, in His infinite wisdom, knew the outcome of Dave's injury, as He knows our beginning and our end. A lot of people serve God, but once a tragedy occurs they tend to drift away from God. It's as if they feel He did them harm or didn't do things according to their plans.

Some may wonder why couldn't God have trusted me with something not physically deforming and painful, like a new car or a raise at work? It's possible that He could; don't get me wrong. But it's in our difficult moments that we can truly understand our strength. In the face of tragedy, the blanket of comfort is removed, and the real test comes into play. God is looking for people to rise above their hurts and remain devoted to Him, even in the challenging moments of life.

Tragedy can cause one to either draw closer to God or move further away. The easy road, for some, would be to turn away, but when you shift your mindset, you consider the difficulty to be an opportunity to grow stronger. God, the Creator of all things, looks into our hearts and knows the outcome of our tragic pain, but ultimately it boils down to how *we* respond. Discovering the positive through hardship can be hard at times. But, as I have learned, it can come in the form of a lesson learned, an opportunity to help others in similar pain, or even gaining a closer relationship with God and others. God knew that He could trust Dave, and upon hearing that statement, it changed everything for him and his ministry. His scars became a platform for him to achieve his destiny. Since that day, he has not battled with suicidal thoughts. Dave's ministry has encouraged millions around the world.[5]

So ask yourself, "What scars has God trusted me with?"

One of Many in a Broken World

When you take a step back and look at the bigger picture of this world, you realize that you are not alone. Everyone is going through difficult life experiences. This can be hard to recognize at times. During my recovery, I spent time alone in my hospital bed with the doors closed, wrapped like a mummy. I felt trapped in my circumstance. To pass the time, I was determined to get on my iPhone. I couldn't use it for the longest time, because I didn't have the physical strength to hit the power button. Talk about being weak! Still, I was desperate to find a way to connect with others in some small way.

With practice, eventually, I could operate my phone. Like most people in their moments of boredom and loneliness, I turned to social media. As I scrolled through my feed, I saw post after post, picture after picture, of how the world was moving on without me. Looking at the pictures, I couldn't help but notice that some people were on vacation, taking in the sunshine, living as if they didn't have a care in the world. I saw others celebrating their weddings or taking walks in the park, and I felt like I was missing out on my life. I had a deep fear that I'd never get to do those things again. There were times when I would find myself frustrated with people as they posted their problems—stuff like a sunburn or not being able to attend a baseball game. My thought was, "You must be joking. You pitiful thing, you." If only I'd had their problems.

But as time went on, I realized I had to mature. You see, in the midst of my situation, I became hardened to other people's problems. Yet, when I began to take my mind off myself, and looked at the big picture, I recognized that those people who were smiling and vacationing, at some point in their lives had encountered difficulty in some form or fashion. In my mind my situation seemed much worse than others', but pain is relative. While I was scoffing at those people, who complained about sunburns and cancelled plans, I'm sure there were others looking at me and scoffing at my complaints of being burned as they dealt with the loss of a loved one.

You gradually see that you are one of many in a broken world. Everyone encounters some sort of scarring event in his or her lifetime. I had to grasp that I wasn't alone. Sometimes the feeling of being alone can hinder the mind-set you need to achieve freedom. What I mean is, if we aren't careful, we can easily develop a "poor me" attitude. In turn, this can cause us to be trapped in self-centered pity, rather than moving on.

Never forget that you aren't alone in your circumstance. Maybe you feel like, "I tried doing good all of my life, and it seems as if life unfairly handed me trouble." But, rest assured, no matter whether I am a good person or a bad person, a Christian or a non-Christian, bad things will happen in this world. *The benefit of being a Christian is that you have an inner hope.*

When bad things happen, we can place our trust in God. When tragedy strikes, not only is it scarring, it can also cause us to lose our motivation to *live again*. I found importance in the discovery of why this trauma was allowed in my life.

Questions for Reflection

Have you ever wondered why trouble occurs in this world?

Throughout your life have you ever said, "WHY ME?"

Do you find yourself relating to my search for answers?

What scars has God trusted you with?

Have you ever felt alone in your circumstance?

*Be sure to sign up at **www.ScarReleaseBook.com** to receive a **FREE study guide** to assist you in walking through your scar-release journey.*

5

TAKE CONTROL
OF THE PROBLEM

"Only I can change my life.
No one can do it for me."
—Carol Burnett[6]

As I was sitting on the edge of my bed in the inpatient rehab, I spent a lot of time meditating on how much my life had been affected by my burns. My body was still wrapped in bandages, aching with pain. My motivation to move on was quickly slipping through the cracks. All of my hopes and dreams were at stake. My life, as I knew it, was gone with the wind.

Doing therapy, day in and day out, was exhausting. At this point, I was doing it only out of requirement, not because

I wanted to. I started to lose the desire to push through the pain because I had suffered enough. It wasn't until I began to read the cards and letters, which I had received from people around the world, that my focus altered. I began to read these stories of how people's lives had been encouraged by something I had done for them before the crash. After the crash, my story grew bigger than I had imagined. People were sending me encouragement letters, telling me to press on. Upon reading these stories, tears rolled down my cheeks. I was immediately touched by seeing the result of the work I had previously done.

I knew that I needed to move on, even if I couldn't do everything as before. I tried to comfort myself by remembering how my story was likely to help others. At that moment, I began to take control of my life. My problems (scars) were now a part of me.

I can't change what happened to me, but I can shift my full attention to bettering my life going forward. To achieve this successfully, I must focus on my improvement.

> "The successful warrior is the average man,
> with laser-like focus."
>
> —Bruce Lee[7]

I get one life. I can allow this tragedy to make me a victim, or I can use this to my benefit to make me a better person. I must find ways to learn from this.

I wanted to live my life and help others through my story. To do that, I needed to take control of my own problems.

Months later, I was living with my family in our hometown of Princeton, where I finally started to heal. The physical scars appeared. I began to understand my limitations, as the scars were contracting and preventing me from moving in the way I wanted. I knew that I needed to have another operation. This would include revisiting the burn unit for more surgery. While I was in the unit, undergoing surgery, my family couldn't go back there with me. They couldn't take my place on that operating table because my family members weren't the ones with the problem.

Obviously, my parents and siblings hurt for me, because I was their son and brother. They knew deep down that I was the one with the burn scars. I was in need of a contracture release. I was the one who had to live with the results. I had to understand just how much I wanted freedom. So maybe you are reading this book, and you can relate to some of these emotional moments. If that's the case, I want to give you some helpful advice that may help you take control of your problem right now.

You must have the desire and drive to see the breakthrough! I have learned with my experience that *you* must be the one who wants it more than anyone else. It is up to you to take the steps in reversing your negative mindset. My advice to you: It's time to take control of your scars, so the scars don't control you!

I want to take another step in my vulnerability. For years I have dealt with something, something that has brought me to tears on many nights. I remember when I was in fourth grade, I noticed how I kept having curse words flow through my mind. These words would come out of nowhere, without warning! As a kid who grew up in church, I knew these curse words were not good things to have floating in my mind. Luckily, I didn't say them out loud for everyone to hear. They were being said silently, in my mind.

Okay, so pause with me for a moment. Can you imagine if, as a kid, I was in a church service, and were to blurt out one of these words at random? Momma would've washed my mouth out with soap! I say this to be funny, because I can laugh about it now, but it was also something very serious that I dealt with daily.

I also started noticing myself performing little rituals, things like obsessive eye-blinking and touching light switches so many times before I could stop. I knew something wasn't right. My mother wasn't a rocket scientist, but she noticed something was wrong. I would go to my parents to discuss these issues. I remember crying to them, telling them that I felt like I had to perform these rituals, otherwise something bad may happen. I found myself worrying nonstop about the safety of my family and myself. My health and the health of others were big concerns to me in the moments of performing these mental rituals.

Through this behavior, I also had found an extreme hatred for germs. Yes, I was, in fact, a germophobe! I couldn't eat the parts of my food that my hand had touched. I always felt dirty. It was so bad, I started eating M&Ms with a spoon!

What kid is afraid to eat M&Ms with their bare hands? My thoughts exactly. I remember spraying the doorknobs of my house with Lysol. My parents knew this was getting out of control. The sad thing is, at this point in my life it got worse. *How could it get any worse?* Well, it did. Finally, my parents took me to the doctor. They explained to the doctor what was happening. He referred me to a psychiatrist.

As a little boy, I remember feeling embarrassed to go see the psychiatrist. What ten-year-old boy would feel happy about it? However, I knew something needed to be done. The psychiatrist diagnosed me with an *extreme* case of obsessive-compulsive disorder (OCD) and Tourette's syndrome. I felt ashamed of my diagnosis. I never wanted to tell anyone about it.

I vividly remember the day that I received my diagnoses. I sat in the chair across from the psychiatrist; my mother was seated in the chair to my left. I asked the doctor a question that was bothering me after receiving the diagnoses. From a young age, I had known that I wanted to go into the ministry to help others. I was plagued with the fear of how this would affect my current and future ministry plans.

My days consisted of daydreaming about the moments I could stand on stage and encourage others. To me, this was extremely important, and I asked the doctor if this would affect my ministry. I will never forget what he said to me: "No, Cody, I think it will enhance your ministry." I was not expecting that answer! My mom, on the other hand, felt goosebumps and knew this was a God-given answer. At the time, what the doctor had said boggled my mind. But weirdly, it gave me hope. As the years went by, I discovered that the doctor was right. I really believed that this disorder was going to enhance my ministry.

When I was in ministry training, I was nineteen years old. During that time, I was given the opportunity to speak at a church service for my classmates. I openly talked about my OCD and Tourette's syndrome in the middle of my sermon. The message ended with an altar call. To my amazement, many of my peers approached me in tears. They shared that they too had dealt with (or were dealing with) similar problems. That very evening after I ministered, memories overflowed of that doctor's response when I was a little boy. "No, Cody, I think it will enhance your ministry." That was confirmation!

As I share this story, I hope you understand that my struggle with OCD and Tourette's was a secret inner conflict that I had been dealing with for years. My mind *is* a constant minefield of chaos at times. It brings so much annoyance. I could let this disorder handicap me to do nothing valuable in this life, but I have chosen to not let it set me back. Instead, I've chosen to use that emotional exhaustion for a greater purpose. It wasn't easy to deal with. At times, it made my life miserable. I would often worry what others would think of me. But the moment that I said this *was not* going to affect my ministry, I took it a step further: I started sharing it with my peers!

I discovered a breakthrough and a sense of freedom in my life. Not only did I receive freedom, but other people started chasing *their* freedom. This all happened as they approached me to discuss their inner battles. Healing was happening in their lives, simply by sharing their hearts and experiences with me. OCD and Tourette's are no longer an embarrassment; rather, I embrace them.

Fear was no longer holding back my life. I saw that it was not affecting my ministry. The doctor's words were correct; this did, in fact enhance my ministry! I share this story to illustrate what taking control of your problem can do. My disorder wasn't going to control my life and ministry. Instead, I took control and used it for the better.

Something powerful happens when we take our lives back. By allowing God to work through my life, I was able to see firsthand how He could work all things together for good.

Taking Back the "Wheel" to Live

In 2014, many months after I had been through intense surgeries and therapy, I needed to make a decision. It involved me getting behind the wheel again. This decision would be a challenging one. Understandably, I was fearful to drive a car again. Driving was an acute, specific trigger that reminded me of why I was scarred in the first place. I could very easily have held off on this and never done it again. However, I ultimately decided I needed to start driving again.

Getting into the driver's seat was hard. Questions raced through my mind. The last time I had driven was the day of the crash. Do I dare get behind the wheel again? What if I get rear-ended again? What if this? What if that? Many thoughts and questions bombarded my mind. I was scared to take that risk again, though I knew deep down that, in order for me to live life and go places, I had to drive again.

Yes, I am permanently scarred, and my scars haven't been removed from my body. They will remain on my body for the rest of my life. The question is, will I allow these scars to keep me from driving again?

I knew I had to take control of my life. At this moment, I was in Indianapolis with my family, and I decided to sit down behind the steering wheel. I put on my seat belt, started the engine, and began to pull out from the parking lot. I slowly started to drive toward the interstate. Upon reaching my destination, I immediately felt relief and was amazed that I had accomplished the task! I had overcome my fear and my scars.

Today, I want to invite you to do the same. Will you ever get behind the wheel again? What's stopping you? Your scars? Scars don't go away, that's why they are scars, but will the scar stop you from getting behind the wheel of your life?

You can't allow fear to control you, because you will

remain complacent and stuck. Don't let your scar be a curse. Let your scar be a blessing! For your scar to be a blessing, you must take action!

Find the Root of Your Problem

To find freedom from a scar, you need to be able to trace the scar back to its root. This process takes place in our minds. Thinking deeply is necessary, but keep in mind that you are only thinking deeply because you want to resolve the problem. I understand that thinking this deeply can be painful. The good thing is we don't have to stay in our pain.

Last year, I went to see my burn surgeon to inquire about surgery. I knew another surgery would bring pain, but it was necessary for me to experience. I had to experience pain if I wanted to see results. I knew the pain would eventually stop. I had to remind myself that I would soon become pain-free. To fix a problem, you must first find the problem and ask how it is affecting your life.

It's possible that you think you already know the root of your scar, but you may not be sure. It is possible that a scar in one area of your life can often lead to another scar elsewhere. If you were abandoned as a child, that abandonment may have left a mark on you. I believe this issue can lead to personal insecurity. It can cause you to question your self-worth or your identity. In some cases, it can lead to depression, anger, confusion, self-loathing, and even suicide. Much like a severe burn, that single injury could lead to many different complications and struggles. To heal, you must understand where your pain originated.

Of course, symptoms of pain and a deep scar may manifest themselves in a less dramatic manner. What about shopping and spending money you don't have? What about the result of becoming a workaholic? Or seeking approval from different circles of people?

Do these behaviors seem bad? Maybe they are not life-ruining, but in the long term we begin to see a pattern unfold. We're longing for validation. It is, deep down, what we all want. Whatever form it comes in, it's something that is ingrained into our DNA. We want to feel complete. Sadly, we receive many scars as children. Painful experiences cause painful memories, and they can lead to a painful life. It's also important to understand that people can be professionals at hiding the pain. They are so good at it that many outsiders (and even family members) have no idea of the hurt that builds inside them. I certainly have had my moments. I can be quick to put on a smile and give a good show.

Unfortunately, behind the scenes, people don't know when I'm unhappy. When I'm in public, my burn scars (depending on what I am wearing) aren't seen by most people. They have no idea that I am a burn survivor, because I cover up everything with so many layers. They may see me in the grocery store and not realize my story—in which I still live. They may not be aware that I nearly died in a horrific crash, and that I carry massive, painful scars from it to this day. They don't know the pain I still carry and go through on a daily basis. I try my hardest and push myself so much for people, but, honestly, if I walk or stand for thirty minutes, the pain becomes unbearable.

The point is, people do not have a clue what others are going through. It's important to show love and respect to those around you. Do you tend to hide your scars? We all hide our pain differently. Just know that it's okay and you're not alone.

To Forgive or Not to Forgive?

I tried, but I couldn't shake feelings about the person driving the refrigerator truck, who had hit me. When he or she decided not to stop at a red light, this careless action cost me my life as I knew it. This individual wasn't under the influence of alcohol or drugs. To this day, I don't know what exactly caused this person to crash into my vehicle. This person was not physically injured in the crash, but the question I've been asked by countless people is whether or not I could find it in my heart to forgive the person who hit me. This has been a rigorous process. In the beginning, I really didn't have much time to think about that person. I was heavily medicated and still going through surgeries. I was fighting to stay alive. But as I began to come out of it, from time to time the driver crossed my mind. I knew that the scars I would carry for the rest of my life were caused by this person's wrongdoing.

Many days of frustration about this individual overwhelmed my mind. Still, I've never met the person, or talked with him or her. Bitterness rooted so strongly that I couldn't enjoy my every day. I needed to take control.

When I finally decided to cross the line of forgiveness, freedom overcame me like a tidal wave. No longer was I going to be bound by this bitterness. Now, this doesn't take away from the fact that I am permanently scarred, and I'm constantly reminded by the physical pain. I just had to make the decision not to allow the scars to grow deeper in my emotions, because frustration ate at me, down to the core, and created bitterness. I realized that it wasn't until I decided to accept my scars that I would be able to take back my life. I would have to stop trying to play the blame game and play the cards that had been dealt to me. That was when I began to see a change in my mobility (perspective).

Do you blame others for your pain? I went through a time when I did. Notice how I said "went through"—I didn't remain stuck. You too can experience this.

To release myself from these scars, I had to forgive the person, which is exactly what everyone should do. My plea is that you grasp the power of forgiveness. In this case, forgiveness equals a breakthrough. In order for me to live a life free from the bonds of these scars, I had to forgive the one who scarred me. My attention is no longer directed at the cause of the scars, but rather on God's deliverance from the scars. The evidence of a breakthrough is when you can talk about your scars not to demean anyone, but to discuss the fact that God has brought you through the challenges that held you back from going further.

My scars are a testimony to how God can deliver you from past hurt caused by a traumatic experience. It would honestly be a wonderful moment for me to some-day meet the individual who crashed into me. More than likely, this crash had to scar him or her emotionally in some way as well. I pray that he or she receives freedom from the scars he or she received that day. I often think, wouldn't it be powerful if God used me to help him or her find their freedom?

Tragedies occur in many different forms. The list can be exhaustive. All traumatic experiences can scar individuals for life. Have you been scarred by another person's wrong-doing or carelessness? Allow me to urge you to practice forgiveness.

Memory of Tragedy

"Scars are memory. Like sutures. They stitch the past to me." —China Mieville[8]

After my accident, not only did I encounter scarring, but my family did as well. Memories of me almost dying continue to haunt their lives.

Let me pull back the curtain. My father, Allen Byrns, is still dealing with the effects of this tragedy. As a dad, he is constantly concerned for me and my brothers. Every time we leave the house, whether we're driving or flying to another location, he exhausts himself over our safety. Now, don't get me wrong, most parents are concerned for the safety of their children, and they should be. However, there is a tipping point when stress can hinder a person's life. It's difficult to know where the exact tipping point lies. I feel it's safe to say that when your stress level is so high that it has an effect on your health and creates an overflow of negativity on the health of your family, you're running into a serious problem.

If I don't text or call my father upon arrival at a location, he panics. He begins to worry to the point that he can do nothing else until he knows that I am okay. This creates an atmosphere that affects my mom and brothers as well. The home fills with frustration and anxiety, and it quickly becomes unhealthy. This is a scar that he is allowing to control his life. He continuously relives the memories of my crash. It prevents him from enjoying his life. The memory has scarred his mind. It limits the peace and joy that he could have.

It's sad that some of us go our entire lives affected by such scars. Are you reliving memories? What moments in your life are producing negative ripple effects? If my dad doesn't take control of his problem soon, it will continue to control him. Are you taking control?

Scars Can Be Infected Easily

As a burn survivor, I am always monitoring my scars because they can easily become infected. I have to pay attention to the chemicals to which I expose my scars. I must be aware of my surroundings at all times, for the sake of my own health.

Just as I have to be careful to avoid infections, you need to be aware of your surroundings, and have this awareness on an emotional level. There are certain things in your life that you know will cause further infection to your scars. But often you choose to sit back and do nothing about them.

You need to be aware of your surroundings. To prevent infection, you need to find a person (or a group of people) with whom you can be open. It's important that you find the right people. If you are constantly around infectious—i.e., negative—people, it can open doors to life-altering complications. One of the most difficult things for me, as someone who has been seen a lot in the public eye, is finding a select group of people with whom I can openly discuss my problems.

Scars that haven't healed are really open wounds. And while it's unfortunate that you can't trust everyone with your open wounds, it's something you need to be aware of. In the beginning stages of my recovery, I had many open wounds on my body, and I was constantly on guard to protect them from infection. If you are dealing with open wounds in your life, be careful of those infectious individuals. They can slow down your healing process.

Now, if someone is messing with a wound who has no business meddling around with it, keep your guard up! During my recovery, I was amazed that everyone suddenly knew how to treat my burn injuries. People with no education in the field somehow magically knew what I needed to do for my healing process. People often think they have all of the answers to your problems. If I can be truthful here, it's quite annoying. When I am dealing with a serious problem, such as burn injury, I don't need a veterinarian telling me what to do.

Whenever I have an operation on my scars, the procedure involves reopening the wound, which causes it to be vulnerable to infection if it not handled properly. In that situation, I need to trust my doctor because of his *qualifications*. When I am in the healing stages, I continue to go back to my *verified* burn surgeon because only he knows how this healing process needs to be treated.

I am sure there are other doctors who can help with this issue, but I would rather be on the safe side. I place my trust in someone who has the experience and the expertise to address my wounds correctly. The point is that when you are trying to get free from the effects of a scar, don't trust just anyone! It's important to find select experts whom you can trust.

Because of my Christian faith, I know for certain of someone I can always trust, and He is Jesus, the ultimate surgeon. My burn doctor also has others working under his authority: nurses, occupational and physical therapists, etc. I've learned that Jesus, too, has people working under *His* authority. In the church, they are known as pastors. *However*, there are times when a certified therapist and other doctors outside of the church *need* to come into the picture. Please hear me: don't be afraid to reach out to professionals beyond the church walls to help you.

When addressing the root of the issue, we expose ourselves. Often when I go to see my surgeon, I have to show him my scars. At first, I had to allow myself to be vulnerable enough, to trust him enough, to show him what my scars looked like. It was a bit scary, to be honest. I have scars on my lower back, my left side, and hip area, which require me to expose some skin, if you know what I'm saying.

I can't just go into the doctor's office with my clothes on and expect him to guess what the scars are doing to my body. I have to be vulnerable. Not only is it difficult for me to expose myself to the surgeon, it's also difficult for me to expose my scars to myself. In the beginning of my recovery, it was hard to look at myself, let alone have someone else come in to look at my scars. I remember many times in the burn unit when I would be taken down to the bath tank to get bathed by the hospital staff. They would lay me in this thing, buck naked, and scrub my wounds while removing hundreds of staples. This was not fun!

To top it all off, an occupational therapist would be ready to start therapy immediately after my scrubbing. I would think, *Could you just wait until I am back in my bandages and my gown, please?* But guess what? No. They wanted to take measurements of my joint mobility and force me to do therapy in an uncomfortable state. I couldn't escape these people. They were everywhere. It was humiliating and frustrating. But deep down, I knew that for my progress it had to be done.

You too need to ask yourself: "Do I want to get better?" If so, you'll just have to accept that you are going to have to take some unpleasant steps to reach your freedom. When I was in the burn unit, I wanted to go home so badly, but it was a process.

As I've said before, even after leaving the burn unit I had to go to an inpatient rehabilitation center. I had to relearn how to walk and care for myself. It wasn't until later that I was stable enough to go home.

When I got home, I felt a sense of freedom. I was ready

to get back to living. My freedom was important to me. When I understood how important freedom was, I knew that nothing would stop me from being able to live freely.

Your Depth Is in Your Why

Recently, at a conference I attended, I was reminded of the importance of asking yourself "why." Dean Graziosi (author and entrepreneurial speaker) was speaking about identifying your "why." He went on to talk about asking yourself "why," to help you get to the root of why you do what you do.

His speech brought back a memory of when I was in middle school. I was riding the school bus, and, of course, I rode the bus with kids younger than myself. These little kids could be annoying at times. They played with the other kids, even us older teens. It required them to ask you a question, and then you to answer, but it would then proceed to them having to ask: "Why?" For example, a kid would ask me, "What is your favorite color?" I would answer: "Purple and blue." They would then ask, "Why?" I would then explain: "I just like those colors." They would then ask again: "Why?" This used to make me so mad! But I learned from Dean that asking this question plays an important role in getting to the root of the issue.

There is a fantastic excerpt from his book, *Millionaire Success Habits: The Gateway to Wealth & Prosperity*, in which Dean writes,

> The issue with most people is that they simply don't go deep enough into their hearts and souls to find out the truth about why they want what they want. It's unfortunate that our brains can so powerfully obscure what's in our hearts and souls.[9]

This was written to help individuals better understand why they wanted wealth and prosperity. But this can apply to other parts of our lives, which is the reason I want to apply this technique to us right now.

"Do you know why you are reading this book?" You may say: "I found the title interesting, or I wanted to read about Cody Byrns' story." Then, I'm going to ask you: "Why? Why is the title interesting? Why do you want to read about me?" Eventually, I would ask you "why" so many times that it would cause you to search and go deeper within yourself to find the answer.

Quite often, we answer with the first thing that comes to mind. But let's go deeper. Why are you reading this book?

Are you scarred? If so, why? What is limiting you in your life? Why do you want freedom?

Once you know your "why," you can then address your problem. Why did I want to go to the surgeon? I wanted to go because I knew that I was limited in my movement, and I wanted the scar cut at the root to allow me to be mobile again. I needed that help in order to be able to hold onto a bottle of water again and juggle better. I wanted to get to the root of the issue. I was tired of going through the motions of therapy. Therapy wasn't working anymore. I needed to see the surgeon. Understanding your "why" will give you the determination you need to live a better life.

Freedom can be yours; however, you will have to go through a healing process. The process can be lengthy and messy, but the results are worth it. After I have surgery, I so badly want my results to be instantaneous. Unfortunately, it doesn't happen that way. Healing takes time. The wound has to heal; stitches have to be removed. Then I have to do therapy, all the while wearing compression garments.

Taking control of the problem will require some action on your part. If you understand the importance of why you are doing it, then your attitude will be conditioned to implement a fresh perspective.

Questions for Reflection

Do you see the importance of taking control?

What is the root of your problem? And how can you take control of it?

Do you need to forgive someone? If so, who?

Are you reliving tragic memories?

What are some moments in your life that could be producing negative ripple effects?

*Be sure to sign up at **www.ScarReleaseBook.com** to receive a **FREE study guide** to assist you in walking through your scar-release journey.*

6

GAIN A FRESH PERSPECTIVE

Sometimes images are the best way to understand something. So, let me paint you a picture:

We have discovered the root of the issue and know that we must take control. Now is the moment we have been waiting for: it's time for the operation. We are going back into the operating room, being transported from the bed onto the operating table. Once on the table, the anesthetist will get to work by injecting a needle into your vein, causing you to drift away into a deep sleep. Before you know it, you wake up and realize the operation is over. You're back in the original room you were assigned to. You are then allowed to leave.

A week or so of healing begins. Then, you are free and healed, ready to go about your merry way. You notice that you feel much better. You feel like a new person after the procedure. You understand that you went into the operating room one way and you have now awakened to a new reality. You have put your old mindset to rest and have gained a new way of thinking. This new mindset is what breaks off the scars of yesterday's troubles. When you think differently, you move differently. I have found this to be key for me on my journey. With my new thought process, I can move freely in my purpose. I can now thrive!

I had to swallow a very bitter pill as I was healing, which is that these scars will always remain on my body. I think that people tend to view them as an awful and ugly part of life; they don't have to be. Scars are, in fact, beautiful! They are proof that you have endured something, and that you have survived.

Unfortunately, society has conditioned us to see ourselves in a certain light. I tried to measure myself using these expectations. So, when looking in the mirror, I hated what I saw. I didn't see myself in the way that society showed me a twenty-three-year-old male should look. I suffered from embarrassment. This new way of life was scary. I had to shift my lifestyle.

I used to love going to the beach. Now, I have to be extremely careful because the sun damages my new skin.

The only thing that helps me move beyond this frustration is to have a new perspective. This only happened when God brought the understanding that I wasn't alone. He showed me how I was supposed to look. I no longer had to measure up to what I saw in the media. Through the support of the service department at The Richard M. Fairbanks Burn Center in Indianapolis, I discovered the Phoenix World Burn Congress. It was there that God showed me His beauty through other burn survivors.

So many individuals who had encountered similar pain and trauma were smiling, laughing, dancing, and living their lives to the fullest. I was inspired. I was moved to tears. I was incredibly grateful to God for opening the door for me to go to this event, because, in that experience, I found community. This event not only challenged me to think about my physical appearance, but my inner self gained restoration. I had to trust that God was revealing the beauty of His plan in my life.

The thing that saddens me the most is that there are some people stuck in their past hurts and experiences. Some people never step into the fullness of what life has to offer. Imagine if you began to look within, and asked yourself this question: "What's holding me back from a better tomorrow?" Let's find it (*the Problem*), give you back your mobility (*the Freedom*), and help you move forward (*Thrive*)! Now, remember that thriving looks different for everyone. For some, it's in their jobs, families, hobbies, life goals, etc. Just as I was shown what thriving looks like, I want to challenge you to figure out how you can thrive today.

The mind is the only thing that can stop us from thriving. We can choose to focus on positive or negative thoughts. Negative thoughts are often byproducts of the television we watch or the things we read in social media or news articles. How can we recognize the positivity in our lives?

I suggest being thankful and counting your blessings. We don't often take the time to appreciate the small things that others may not have, like a bed and a hot meal, being able to walk—being able to see or smell. The list goes on, but these are just some of the small things we can focus on. For me, as a Christian, going to church, being devoted to my prayer life—these are encouraging and uplifting practices that keep me focused. They are how I continue to strive for a positive mindset.

Stepping into Awareness

Many times, we hear negative thoughts like, "I am doomed. I can't live a successful life." I believe this kind of negative thinking is brought about by spiritual warfare. As a Christian, I believe that there is an enemy, the devil. He wishes to destroy God's creation. I believe that the enemy wants to attack by whispering lies to keep us distracted from the truth. The enemy can sometimes use negative media to distract us from the truth. The media is so loud that we often cannot escape the noise. These distractions have the platform to produce the kind of negative thoughts I've mentioned.

I believe that the enemy will tell a lie long enough to try to convince the world to believe it. In my opinion, the enemy would love for me to give up on God altogether. When negative thoughts would arrive in my mind—*What did I do to deserve this?* Or, *Why me?*—I could have been stuck with a bitter mindset. I've met many people who have been so affected by negative thinking that it rubs off on others around them, such as their spouse, children, coworkers, etc. When we live our lives with a pessimistic viewpoint, we can sometimes limit ourselves from receiving God's blessings around us. Have you ever found yourself consumed by so much negativity that it limits you from experiencing joy? Maybe you can relate to this because it's affecting your life now. If so, I promise you it will get better.

For me, it's essential to spend time with God and privately

express the struggles in my life. I've talked to Him about my physical and emotional scars, the ones that have been holding me back from doing great things in life. Through this, I have found myself feeling a sense of freedom. The amazing thing is that God is continually exposing built-up things that have been hindering me from living a better life. God knows us better than we know ourselves. The catch is that we must call out to Him. Remember: humanity was designed to have a relationship with God. When you begin to connect with your Creator, healing begins.

I cannot begin to tell you how many times I've cried during my appointments with God. As I start to express one thing, I sense myself talking to Him about other things. Talking about your problems can be beneficial. Some people find that writing down their pain and hurts is a helpful way to discover their freedom.

Juggling Perspective

Due to my burn injuries, I lost the ability to juggle the way I once could. Before the crash, I was very skilled in my juggling abilities. I professionally juggled all kinds of random objects. I had been juggling since I was nine years old. In early 2013, I was able to juggle seven balls, eight hoops, five flaming torches, large knives, and pretty much anything I could get my hands on. I loved to juggle! I didn't even need an audience to enjoy myself. I genuinely loved it. But when the crash happened, my hands were completely burned.

My family members remember that while I was in a coma the surgeon informed them that they possibly would need to amputate three of my fingers. My family quickly responded: "No! He juggles!"

Of course, you can imagine the look on the surgeon's face. He probably thought, "You've got to be kidding me?" Still, they did everything in their power to save my fingers. But, due to the severe burn injuries, those fingers don't bend and move as they did before.

Let's fast-forward to the time I was in the rehab facility. I was trying to walk and use my hands again. One day, I was blessed by a visit from some fellow jugglers. In the moment of their checking in on me and my progress, I wanted to see if I could juggle. At that time, I still couldn't walk, and I was only able to sit on the side of my bed. As I finished positioning myself, they handed me three beanbags. My hands were wrapped in bandages, and I had splints and pins inside my fingers. Understandably, I couldn't manipulate objects with my hands. This was heartbreaking, after spending years perfecting the skill and even getting paid to juggle for audiences. Suddenly, I couldn't do it anymore.

My friends left me the three beanbags as motivation to reteach myself. Weeks later, after learning to stand and walk on my own, I knew I needed to at least try to juggle again. Juggling was no longer a smooth, fun experience for me. It was hard and incredibly frustrating. I remember being determined one minute, and then angry and wanting to give up the next.

Deep down, there was still a little boy in me who was determined to juggle. So, of course, I couldn't give up. I can now juggle six balls! A few days ago, I was almost able to juggle seven balls again. I'm not there yet, but it's a start.

I also mentioned how I used to juggle things besides beanbags, such as eight hoops. I have since worked my way up to five hoops! My fingers can't bend correctly, so I am unable to hold the other three hoops to get them in the air. I lost the ability to juggle all eight hoops because of my injuries. Nonetheless, I am thankful that I can juggle five hoops again. I mean, come on, that is impressive, right? Most people can't do three. The moral of the story is I lost something because of my injuries. I lost three of those eight hoops that I used to juggle.

What can those three hoops represent in *your* life? What are those things in your life that you once had but now don't? A marriage? A loved one? A career? A hobby? Have you given up on pursuing your goals and dreams because of what you've lost? Let me challenge you: pick up the five things that you do have, and don't allow the other three things that you've lost to keep you stuck. You want to be able to function in life.

I will never forget the three other hoops I could once juggle. You will never forget the things that you've lost. The fact is that life must go on. You can't forget about the five things that you do have. It's important to have a positive perspective, because that is when you can produce a positive outcome.

Questions for Reflection

Has your perspective on life been negative? If so, how are you going to change that?

Do you often find media creating your perspective?

Name some things or people you can appreciate today.

What's holding you back from a better tomorrow?

What does thriving look like to you? How can you thrive today?

*Be sure to sign up at **www.ScarReleaseBook.com** to receive a **FREE study guide** to assist you in walking through your scar-release journey.*

7

BEGIN THERAPY

Many times, in our moments of pain and hurt, we are focused on our own problems. As I've mentioned, when we're caught up in our own pain, we tend to fail to realize that others are hurting as well. This is something I had to recognize.

Some people are in more pain than you. Truth be told, sometimes the best medicine is to serve others in the midst of your pain. Often, we will discover that we don't have it so bad after all. When I was in the burn unit, I was told that two other patients had died due to their injuries. I almost died multiple times in the unit, due to lack of oxygen, pneumonia, becoming septic, and other complications. But guess what? I am alive! So, who am I to complain about my problems?

Do you catch my drift? Once again, when we step out of our daily circle of self, we begin to see that there are others who need help. When you start to help others, you begin to experience a real sense of therapy and healing.

> *True therapy takes place*
> *when we can help others around us.*

Occupational Therapy

During my rehabilitation days, I formed friendships with my therapists. I fell in love with these individuals. Instead of focusing on the pain, which would be challenging at times, I wanted to keep my focus on the positive aspects of the situation. My therapists were a joy to work with, one woman specifically. She and I became good friends on my journey to recovery. It got to the point that I was excited to do my therapy because I had made a friend. This woman was fun to be around, and intuitive in her profession.

Something I found helpful during this time was that she would always ask how I was doing, and I would ask her how she was doing. I decided to make my therapy appointments a time when I could receive professional therapy, while also asking her about her day and trying to uplift her. I would, on occasion, bring her coffee, which let her know that I appreciated her.

Hopefully, God revealed His love to her in those moments. The more I did this, the more I felt myself being uplifted. She is a hardworking therapist, with a wonderful husband and two adorable children. She too has a life. I wanted to use that time as an opportunity to help encourage her. I hope and pray that God continues to bless her and her family.

The moral of the story is that I realized that the more I could help others, the quicker I would recover. This motivated me, and remains my motivation. I am still here on this earth for a reason, and so are you! You weren't born just to be born. Take hold of the opportunity you have in front of you. If I had never taken control and retrained my thinking while actively helping others, I could be in a bar somewhere, drinking my life away, feeling hopeless and bound by bitterness. But I refuse to live my life that way.

The Importance of Staying Positive

It is possible for our old ways of thinking to arise again. In the same way, after a surgical release on my contracture scars, if I don't work to stretch and massage my scars after the procedure, it is possible for those scars to contract into the very same positions they were in before. Remember the importance of daily therapy. You must continually keep focused on the positivity of your situation.

If I am not careful, I can easily find myself thinking negatively about my predicament, which can lead to being stuck all over again. I don't want that! But the moment those thoughts try to arise, I merely refocus my attention on the positive and immediately begin to thank God for the things I have and for His mercy and grace.

It's a lifelong commitment. It can be challenging at times, but it is rewarding. I don't think I can stress this enough: you must stay committed. To be honest, it has been challenging for me to hold onto these truths every day. It's tempting to put this thought process on the back burner, so to speak. When we do this, we can slowly start falling into a delusion, to the point that we ignore the steps that we need to take to remain free from our past scars.

Once again, you must remind yourself daily *why* you want to be free. Even if you have to place post-it notes in your home, vehicle, or office, you need to remember the importance of living a life of freedom. The more you do this, the more you will stay on track and be successfully released from your scars.

Compression Garments

Let's once again travel back to my critical stages, after receiving skin grafts. Just as the healing process starts, it's extremely important that I obey the instructions of the surgeon and his team. As these scars are healing, they are constantly being wrapped in bandages, due to draining fluid and blood. Now, as the fluid lessens, they begin to take measurements for compression garments.

Fresh scar tissue takes time to mature. Contracture scars can take six to eight months to mature, and during this process I was required to wear compression garments. These garments were to help smooth out the scars.

I will never forget when I learned that I had to wear these garments. I was on a moving bed, inside the therapy department in the burn unit. They brought me garments; more specifically, gloves. They shared with me that I was now required to wear them. I thought, *How am I going to juggle and perform in these?*

I realized I would have to cancel all of my speaking events for the rest of the year. There was no way, with the compression garments, as my body worked to heal itself, that I was going to be able to juggle. It was a hard and tragic realization for me, but when I accepted what I needed to do to heal properly, I was able to move forward, albeit slowly.

The compression garments were specially made for my body. I eventually had to wear a full-body outfit—nothing but compression. The first compression suit I had was blue, and when I wasn't wearing any other clothes, I still had my tight compression suit on. I felt as though I was a disfigured Clark Kent. Seriously! I felt as though I was wearing a Superman costume. What if I had run into the grocery store, taken off my outer clothes to show off my Superman garments underneath, and pretend to save the day? I've had many daydreams about this. I learned to laugh and be cheerful during my healing process. "A cheerful heart is good medicine, but a crushed spirit dries up the bones." — Proverbs 17:22 (NKJV).

Another funny story is when I would sleep at night in my compression suit, I would often wake up to a large, blue stain on my bedsheets. Great. It looked like the scene of a Smurf murder (Sorry, Mom!).

Anyway, back to the point. I knew that if I wanted my scars to age well and correctly smooth out, I needed to wear these garments, day and night, for the next eight months. Due to my fingers and hands being burnt, it was often a challenge just to put these garments on. Thank God, my family was there to assist me with this. Still, to this day, I have to wear compression garments, especially after I undergo surgery.

After one has been released from their scar(s), they too need to apply compression. Compression for an emotional scar is applied when you practice the discipline(s) to achieve the results you want. It's a matter of choosing to take those hard steps. We already know that they will make us better in the long run, but we still have to fight our desire not to do the work. My compression garments weren't fun to wear, but I wore them because I knew they were going to help with my healing. Therapy requires us to get out of our comfort zone.

What Does Being Healed Look Like?

This question is one that often brings debate. My belief is that these outward scars are proof that the body has healed physically to the best of its ability. When you can move in freedom where the inner pain was, that's when you have succeeded. Again, I am writing this book for you from a Christian's point of view, and as someone who has suffered from severe, life-threatening injuries. I believe I am healed, but others may argue with my opinion, and that's okay. My reason for saying that I am healed is more emotional. However, on the outside, I am medically stable and strong enough to be considered recovered. But to some I am not, because of my outward appearance. They may say, "Well, if Jesus healed people by making the blind see, and the lame walk, etc., why are you still carrying scars and pain?" Through Isaiah 55:8-9, I choose to cling or stand on this truth as a promise of God's spoken Word:

"For My thoughts are not your thoughts, Nor are your ways My ways," says the Lord. "For as the heavens are higher than the earth, So are My ways higher than your ways, And My thoughts than your thoughts" (NKJV).

The reality is God knows what's best, and only He knows. He can see the big picture of my life. Can Jesus perform miracles? Absolutely! I have heard stories of how God healed people with physical and internal evidence. *But what if these things don't happen for others?* We need to trust God when we don't have all of the answers.

Something else I've found with my scars is that since they don't go away, they often remind me of my dependency on God. These markings remind me how much God has brought me through, and also shows me to never forget what He has done for me. Throughout my life, I have been presented with many opportunities to become boastful, but the benefit of my new appearance is that it keeps me humble and yet grateful to God for allowing me to live the life I have. This is something I've found beneficial in regard to my physical appearance. When I think from a Godly perspective, the most important healing isn't so much physical. It is, in fact, emotional healing. Healing within your mind is necessary, as it's connected to your soul, which brings about spiritual healing. Your soul is the most important thing in this life. On this earth, I will carry permanent scars for the rest of my life. (I'm not saying that Jesus can't remove my scars, because He certainly can.) Even if I do go the rest of my life with physical scars, I am not allowing my scars to remove me from my relationship with God, nor am I letting these scars limit me in my life.

Finding Role Models

Throughout my journey, I have found encouragement by looking at the lives of others around me. There are many role models who've inspired me in my moments of hardship. Some of these individuals are now personal mentors and dear friends whom I will forever cherish.

One lady comes specifically to mind, but for the sake of her privacy I won't mention her name. This woman used to mentor me in my clown makeup. Yes, I said clown makeup. When I was a child, I became heavily involved in clown ministry. Not every kid my age wanted to be a clown. Most wanted to be an athlete or a musician. But there was, at the time, an adult clown troupe that actively participated in clown ministry. A few ladies from the troupe took me under their wing to help me, one of whom was this particular lady. She is incredibly talented. Not only is she a professional clown, but she is also a professional artist, musician, and writer. She also taught others such as myself her talents. This lady's journey hasn't been an easy one.

Unfortunately, she's battled multiple problems in her life. One was cancer. What's interesting is she didn't tell the world about this issue, but she found trustworthy people to pray for her. In spite of this difficulty, she never stopped pursuing her God-given calling. Her calling was connected to her talents, as she persistently helped others and continued to set goals for herself.

After much prayer and proper dieting, she is healed of cancer! She now lives a fulfilling lifestyle and shares her story to bring honor and glory to God. Talk about inspiring. Life handed her something tragic, but she didn't lose hope. This is encouraging, and I am sure that she found helping others in her own moment of discomfort to be therapeutic. She is an example and role model for me, as she lives her life helping others. In my journey, I have found such importance in helping people. Who can you help today?

Questions for Reflection

The greatest therapy is helping others. Who can you help today?

Do you have any role models? If so, who?

*Be sure to sign up at **www.ScarReleaseBook.com**
to receive a **FREE study guide** to assist you in
walking through your scar-release journey.*

8

EMBRACE YOUR STORY

Sunday, September 15, 2013

There I was, standing on a stage in my home church. The crowd was standing and applauding my arrival. I couldn't believe that all of these people were celebrating my story of recovery: first responders, news reporters, family, and my church family. I was so nervous, yet so thankful to see the faces of those who had been cheering me on. As the crowd began to sit back down, I started to express my gratitude. I thanked everyone for their support, especially the first responders, for doing what they did. It meant the world to me, giving me the chance to live again.

After giving thanks, I pulled out an old suitcase that held three juggling balls. Now, the crowd wasn't expecting this, due to my injuries and my apparel. Keep in mind that

I was wearing a full upper-body brace and a full body-compression suit with multiple layers of bandages underneath. My hands were wrapped, and I had three pins in my fingers. Call it what you want, but I had worked very hard to regain my ability to juggle three balls again. I wanted to perform and show off my success.

As the crowd waited anxiously, I began to juggle—and they roared with excitement! Before the injury I had juggled seven balls, and the truth is I'd never received applause like that. I was utterly baffled by it. I had won awards for my showmanship and I was now only juggling three balls? I believe it boiled down to this: I now had a story to go along with my skills. Now when people understand my story, they are even more amazed at my juggling than before. Why? Because my scars show strength and make me different from other jugglers. Don't get me wrong; I am the world's best juggler—according to my mom (thanks, Mom!).

This moment of celebration is one I need to carry with me every day. The very fact that I am alive is a reason to celebrate. May I never forget this experience. It was at that moment when I began to embrace my story.

Have you ever fully embraced your story? What's done is done; I can't change it. There is an importance to embracing this fact. I did, nonetheless, survive a horrific event. Our scars are proof that we have endured and overcome. We don't have to like the pain we've suffered, but we do need to practice moving past it.

We must embrace our stories and find ways to celebrate the now. You are a precious gift to our world. You are unique and you have your own story. The very fact that you are breathing now is something to rejoice about! Your scars are your own, representing your survival. Now that you have survived, let's begin the process of thriving!

Scars Are an Upgrade

A good friend and mentor, Dr. Sean Stephenson, was born with a genetic disorder called osteogenesis imperfecta, commonly known as "brittle bone disease." He is an excellent example of a person who has not allowed circumstances to keep him in bondage. His career has been remarkable and even led him to work in the White House under President Bill Clinton.[10] He and I were discussing the topic of scars. As we were talking, he began to share how our scars are an upgrade.

To Dr. Stephenson, his physical appearance is a badge of honor. He has gone through so many hurdles, but remains determined to help others with his mission of "Ridding the World of Insecurities." Dr. Stephenson is someone who has risen above challenges. He doesn't allow them to hinder his goals in life. His confidence and strength came about because of his hard work and outlook on life. *Yesterday's* troubles can bring about *tomorrow's* respect. It's all a matter of how you handle yourself *today*. That's what will make the difference.

Since receiving my scars, I've noticed something. I suddenly have people offering me respect in ways they didn't before. My ministry suddenly expanded to every age group and to others beyond the church walls. My speaking career has also gained access to the burn-survivor community across the country.

As I turn my attention to the Bible, I read about many people who deal with scars. But amazingly, they didn't allow their scars to stop them from achieving their God-given purpose. Instead, their arduous journeys put them on the path to experiencing their destinies. We learn of a man named Joseph, who you can read about in Genesis chapters 37-50. I will give a brief synopsis of his story and show why there is a connection.

He had eleven brothers and a dad who highly favored him over the rest. Joseph had a dream that his brothers would someday bow down to him. He told this to his brothers, and out of jealousy his brothers threw him into a pit and left him for dead. I'd imagine this was a scarring event for him. Later, his brothers removed him from the pit and sold him into slavery. He eventually ended up in jail. Talk about a rough journey. While he was in prison, news spread about a unique gift that Joseph had, as he could interpret dreams.

At the time, the king was called pharaoh. Pharaoh encountered some bad dreams and sought answers for what they meant. Eventually, word got to Pharaoh about Joseph. Joseph had the privilege of explaining the dream. Doing this led him to become second-in-command to the King. It was a big promotion, from prisoner to second-in-command. This would then put Joseph in the position for his vision to come to pass, as his brothers did end up bowing down to him in their time of need. Joseph didn't allow unforgiveness to prevent him from helping them. Do you see how this troublesome journey put Joseph on the path to accomplishing his purpose?

I find myself relating to Joseph because when I was a little boy I knew without any doubt that God was calling me to help people. Then, on June 19, 2013, I found myself waking from a coma and severely burned. I hadn't seen that coming, and I imagine Joseph probably thought the same thing as he was being thrown into the pit. But looking back, it has helped me to become a better man, and it has also enhanced my dream of helping people. It may not have been exactly how I imagined it, but it has helped put me on the path that I've always seen myself on. I feel as though God has taken this horrible experience and created something beautiful from it.

Could it be that your suffering might produce your dream? This journey has brought forth distress, but I am grateful for the life I have. As I mentioned, I now consider my scars to be an upgrade. My life has been taken to another level because I learned the valuable lessons that only pain could teach me.

This experience hasn't prevented me from enjoying life. I am living as an overcomer. Something I've learned is when you live with an overcomer perspective, you can attract people, too, because they will want what you have. People find this behavior pleasing to be around. Many have been drawn to my story. It sparks interest in people, because I am still a Christian with a positive attitude, in spite of this tragedy.

People often think Christians serve God because of what He can do for them; "He makes their lives perfect," or so they think. But they look at the hand I was dealt, and I am still serving God. Being a Christian is not about living a life of perfection without problems. That's not true at all. When the rubber hits the road, we suffer for our beliefs, and we aren't always popular with those around us. We aren't promised a comfortable life. Granted, as a Christian, I believe in having eternal life in heaven, which is going to be amazing. But life on earth isn't easy.

People are searching for their purpose. Unfortunately, there are some who have given up on searching and who remain numb. They will typically go through their lives trying to fill the void with the next best drug or high. Finding your purpose doesn't have to be hard. Let me give you some helpful insight: the moment you can help someone else is the moment you activate your purpose.

Purpose is awaiting you! Imagine a car parked in a parking lot. Maybe it encountered some dents and scratches in the past, and because of this it has remained parked for years. But that vehicle still has the potential to be driven. If someone started up the engine, they would recognize that it's still got value. Maybe, just maybe, they would decide to hit the road again.

Before the car can take off, one must know where it's going. Luckily, there is a GPS system. Let's say I wanted to drive to Los Angeles from Tampa where I live now. The reality is, I am not going to get there overnight by car. It's going to require some time and effort. But I at least know my destination. It's typed into the GPS.

I need to get this car on the road and begin my journey. As I take off toward LA, I'm going to find that there are some busy roads and some seldom-driven roads. I may even miss a few turns, and I may need to reroute myself, but the important thing is to not lose focus on the destination. Maybe I continue my drive and I run out of gas. I need to find a gas station. Or let's say my tire goes flat and I need air in my tire. These obstacles can appear, but they will not prevent me from arriving in LA.

Finally, I hit LA and I've made my destination! Hooray! The car did it! Now, I shared this story to say that this vehicle may represent you. Maybe you have been sitting for your whole life in one spot, settling on your reality, afraid to go any further in fulfilling your purpose. Guess what? You still have potential to accomplish great things.

I want to challenge you to find your destination (purpose) and begin your journey. Don't let the scratches or dents that you've encountered in the past stop you from setting new goals for yourself. Keep in mind that bumps in the road will always occur.

You may miss a few turns, but don't stop your journey. You are going to get there. You may run low on gas, but, be encouraged, there is a gas station down the road. In our world, there are many opportunities to fuel yourself with the right fuel to motivate you to keep going. It's possible that you will get a flat tire, but keep in mind that there is a truck stop that can assist you in fixing it. This truck stop may represent a conference, or even a Bible study group.

Whatever it may be, other people can help you on your journey. Before you know it, you will arrive, and the journey doesn't stop there. Continue setting goals for yourself. Don't give up on living life and helping others along the way. This, to me, is success.

Do you find yourself wanting to live a successful life?

> "The key to success is playing the hand you were dealt like it was the hand you wanted."
> —Kaitlyn Walsh[11]

That quotation packs a punch! If I sum up this chapter in one sentence: I refuse to allow this tragedy to stop me from living a fulfilled life. No matter what happens in this life, you can still rise above your circumstances and use them to your benefit. Use those scarring moments as stepping stones to elevate yourself to a higher platform. Another quote I find enjoyment from is:

"An arrow can only be shot by pulling it back. So when life is dragging you back with difficulties, it means that it's going to launch you into something great. Just focus and keep aiming!"

—Unknown[12]

When you are released from yesterday's troubles, as mentioned in this quote, you become an arrow in a bow. The arrow has been pulled back, but it only enhances the distance of how far it will go. The crash set me back some, but my launch to success has been greater.

Questions for Reflection

How can you embrace your story today?

What are some ways you can consider your scars as an upgrade in life?

How do you define success?

In what ways could your scars assist you in achieving success?

*Be sure to sign up at **www.ScarReleaseBook.com** to receive a **FREE study guide** to assist you in walking through your scar-release journey.*

9

LIVE ABUNDANTLY

Another word for "abundant" is "plentiful." In light of this, we need to understand that living abundantly includes being generous.

Generosity comes in many forms, not just in financial terms. Think of it as uplifting others through your story, living a healthier lifestyle for your spouse and children, expressing thankfulness, or producing a positive atmosphere for others. These are all ways that we can be generous. Another way to conceive abundance is in the word "overflowing." Think about the overflowing hope you can give to others in their times of need.

What about the family down the street that is suffering from trauma? Living abundantly is when we can extend the lessons we've learned to others. You contain a message that is born through your story and experiences. How can you package that message to bless others? Maybe it's sending a letter of encouragement to someone, or even inviting someone to lunch. It's all about extending a helping hand to others with your message.

Living in abundance occurs when we live a life that no longer revolves around ourselves and our wants. Think about the impact that you can make! It's amazing to see the ripple effect that freedom can have on someone's life. Your freedom allows others to access love and hope. The more you thrive, the more you will recognize the gifts that you are providing to the world.

The Benefits of A Scar

Dr. Dave Roever mentioned something I believe we can all find helpful. Roever shares:

> A scar is proof that you have been damaged or hurt, but a scar comes back stronger and tougher, and you can experience more hurt in the future without hemorrhaging to death because that scar is going to pay you back.

He also states these three things specifically about a scar: number one, a scar is evidence you've gotten hurt; number two, it's evidence that you've gotten over it; and number three, it's evidence of empathy. When you begin to share your personal story and experience with others who are hurting, it is great therapy for you and for the listener. As Dave shared, your scars can be evidence that you've gotten hurt and made it through, which brings encouragement to others. You can indeed take the worst of tragedies and turn them into a lesson for someone else. I wonder how many people could benefit from hearing your story.[13]

Blessings

I can honestly say that my burn injuries have opened a door for me to be a blessing in a way that I never imagined they could.

A few months ago, I was invited to speak at a conference in Madison, Wisconsin. The conference attendees all had something in common: they were all burn survivors. As a speaker, I was excited to have this opportunity. Upon my arrival, I quickly got a ride to my hotel and settled in for the weekend. I was scheduled to speak the next morning. After starting my morning, I approached the crowd, and I quickly began sharing my story, adding some humor and juggling. This was so much fun! I finished my keynote and took my seat. After that session, multiple attendees expressed their thanks and gratitude for my sharing. A few of these survivors approached me in tears, as they were so appreciative of my words. These moments, to me, were therapeutic on many levels, as I not only had the honor and privilege of helping to encourage others with my story, but I too was encouraged.

Need I remind you that these attendees were burn survivors themselves. It's a fantastic accomplishment when you can overcome your scars to encourage others who are battling their own similar scars. You have the ability, because your story can bring hope to others. Interestingly, there are times when only your personal story can help someone else, because they are battling or have battled similar experiences. Burn injuries provided a particular connection at this conference. It opened the door for the message to be accepted.

How can you be a blessing to others? In today's society, we are in desperate need of men and women who are willing to not give up because of the hardships they encounter—people who have been scarred, but who are not stuck in their scars. I believe that God has truly blessed me. He has supplied me with the tools and resources to bless others through starting a burn foundation.

I get to help others who have gone through the same kind of tragedy I encountered. The burn surgeon whom God used to save my life, Dr. Rajiv Sood, is a tremendous individual who has spent the last twenty-five years helping over 7,000 burn patients. His wisdom and accomplishments are highly admired in the field of burn healing. He has decided to voluntarily provide his skills and knowledge as a surgeon to help the burn survivors involved with The Cody Byrns Foundation, which is amazing in itself.

The Foundation's goal is to help provide the funds for reconstructive surgeries to burn survivors who are in desperate need of these procedures. These procedures are often very costly, and insurance companies will only pay so much for them, often leaving survivors stuck in their circumstances. The Foundation wants to go the extra mile, providing funds for these surgeries to take place. With these procedures, we want to help burn patients who are in need, nationally and internationally. We will not only help these patients by providing financial assistance with the hospital fees, but we'll also transport them to The Richard M. Fairbanks Burn Center in Indianapolis, under the direction of Dr. Rajiv Sood. We are also planning to provide the financial assistance for one other family member of the patient to have a hotel during the patient's recovery.

The Foundation will provide gift baskets to the patient and family member. Each basket will be filled with gift cards, snacks, and other helpful resources. We will also include a Bible—and *this book you are reading today*! Cody Byrns Ministries, Inc. will be assisting The Cody Byrns Foundation with raising the needed funds by offering burn-awareness information and inviting donors to give through my speaking engagements and fundraising events.

In short, the Foundation's goal is to equip other survivors with the proper resources to further enhance their recovery. Do you see how my freedom is now blessing others? My scars provided an open door to help others who are suffering from similar injuries. You may be the answer to someone's prayer.

Never Be Ashamed

When you look at yourself, you may not feel qualified to share your story. But you *are* qualified! Your story is your story! When the opportunity arises for you to share your scars with others, don't be ashamed! You are an example to others.

When I go to speak somewhere, I often share a slide-show of images of the crash and the damage to my body. This helps those in attendance to understand the full impact of my injury. When they see me onstage, my scars are covered with clothing. But the moment I reveal the scars to them, I gain their attention. Their attention then gives me the opportunity to share something of value that can help them in their lives. You can apply this to your story, too; maybe not with visual images, but in your own unique way. Be confident in yourself! The more confidence you have, the more you will shine!

Confidence often attracts people. One of the things I learned in my performing days is that the moment I get on stage, I must project confidence in myself and my ability to control the crowd and keep them entertained. When I am confident, the audience senses this, and they become attracted to what I have to offer. In our lives, we need to be content with who we are as individuals.

Life Is but a Mist

"What is your life? You are a mist that appears for a little while and then vanishes" (James 4:14, NIV). Life is but a mist. Imagine spraying a can of Lysol. One spray equals one mist. Watch how quickly that mist evaporates. The life we have on this earth isn't long, my friends. As a young man, I was exposed to this reality. I was twenty-three years old when that truck crashed into me. I wasn't doing anything wrong, but sitting at a stop light on the highway. Life very quickly could have ended for me that day. When I was a child, growing up in the church, I would always hear pastors say we aren't promised tomorrow. I now understand how truly short this life is. We must make the most of every day we're given.

When we truly begin to understand just how short life is, we can start to see how important it is that we make the most of our today. My body went from being non-scarred to scarred in the year 2013. I had to decide to not allow this to affect my calling on earth. Once again, I let it enhance my calling. You too can apply that to your own life! I want to encourage you to make the most of your time on earth. How can you make a positive impact on the world we live in with the scars you carry?

You can make a difference! Think about all that you can provide to our society. How you live your life is a message to others. I wonder how many people watch you on a day-to-day basis who could benefit from your actions. After the crash, I had many eyes watching my actions, including hundreds of children's. This was the moment I needed to practice what I preached, not so much with my words, but with my actions. The way I handle myself in the face of tribulation shows others who I am at the core.

> "Preach the Gospel at all times, and if necessary use words."
>
> —Francis of Assisi[14]

Shortly after I made my first appearance at my home church, I walked outside the sanctuary doors to find a little boy running to me with tears in his eyes. He wrapped his arms around me and buried his head in my stomach. This was the moment I knew that my actions mattered. Through his coming to me in tears, I realized how much I meant to these children. I knew that my actions in the midst of tragedy were setting an example. God had taken one of the worst experiences of my life and used it to help others.

If nothing else that you read in this book sticks with you, please remember this: You may be stuck now, but freedom awaits you! I want you to experience a good life, one that is free from being stuck in bondage! You must be free to be you, to walk in your God-given purpose, and to accomplish your goals and dreams. Maybe you started out on the right road toward those passions, but somehow got scarred or possibly bound. As a result of being stuck, you gave up on the journey you were designed for. But don't you dare think for a moment that it's too late to go after those dreams! Once you have your scar released, you will begin to move faster than ever before!

Questions for Reflection

What are some ways you can be a blessing to others?

Who could benefit from your positive actions?

*Be sure to sign up at **www.ScarReleaseBook.com** to receive a **FREE study guide** to assist you in walking through your scar-release journey.*

CONCLUSION

It is my honor and pleasure to write this book for you. By God's miraculous power and His saving grace, I am alive to share my experience and knowledge. It's a blessing for me to share this information with you, yet I also feel that this is a responsibility given to me by God.

I believe that God wants to reveal some things to you through my personal story, combined with metaphors, so that I can relate it to you on a personal level and, most importantly, share God's word. With these ingredients, I hope and pray you are better equipped to live a life of freedom.

As we reach the end of this book, my prayer and hope is that you have discovered a clearer understanding of what a scar is and how it is formed, as well as an understanding of whether you have emotional scars that are holding you back from living a full life. Hopefully, by now, you have begun to take the steps to achieve your freedom! You have learned about my story and the contracture scars that I deal with as a burn survivor. *You have learned that a scar release doesn't remove the appearance of a scar, but allows mobility to move with the scar.*

Not only was the procedure essential, but so was my daily therapy after the procedure. We connected the dots to discover how strong scars can keep us in bondage and have a negative effect, as well as discover that scars can enhance our lives positively, after we have been freed from them. God can use our story to help others find freedom. Today, as you conclude this scar-release journey we've taken together, I want to encourage you to put this book in a location that will not collect dust. Instead, pass this information along to someone whom you believe could be helped by it.

Most importantly, you now have the message inside you! So, share it with the world in the way you live! May God bless you in your life as you step out of bondage and into a life of freedom and abundance! Let's make a difference! I love you so much! To God be the glory! Until next time, let's enjoy life!

DO YOU WANT
TO KNOW JESUS?

Being found lifeless in a vehicle that was engulfed in flames is still difficult to grasp. According to the first responders and photos taken by the sheriff's department, my vehicle looked like a scrunched-up accordion. The first responders were confident that no one could survive such a crash. I was considered dead. It wasn't until my hand moved that they realized the importance of rescuing me. Interestingly enough, the responders said that I was talking! I was able to tell them who I was and where I worked.

As I said earlier in the book, I do not recall any of this happening. I have *no* memory of the crash. I was burning alive inside a vehicle and I couldn't get out, even if I had been coherent enough to try. I was literally squashed inside a deformed SUV, trapped in a horrific situation. The fire department used the jaws of life to help free me from the wreckage.

Months later, after I was released from the hospital, the local fire department shared their experience of the crash with me. Many of them tearfully expressed that this tragedy had made an incredible impact on their lives. It was recorded as one of the worst accidents ever within my local community. If they had not seen my hand move, I would've been burnt alive! No doubt at all.

Since I have no memory of this experience, I believe with all of my heart that God took control of my hand. To this day, God is still in control. With all of that said, the community was amazed I was still alive. Imagine how your friends, family, and coworkers would react when they saw you standing, alive with a purpose and a passion for accomplishing your dreams. People will be shocked! I've had people say to me, "Cody, you are like a real-life terminator! You don't see people survive crashes like that, except in the movies." I laugh and my response is, "It's the power of God!"

God has continued to amaze me as I have gone through this tragedy. He has elevated me to a level I thought I would never achieve. God can elevate you, too.

Today, you can know Jesus, and He can set you free, not

just from scars but also from the bondage of sin and death. Over 2,000 years ago, God sent His Son, Jesus, to die on a cross so that you and I could be forgiven for our sins and have the opportunity to know Him personally. He didn't die because He was weak. Instead, He stayed on the cross to bear the punishment we deserved for our sins, which was death. He loves us, my friend. The Bible tells us that Jesus rose again three days after His death. He is alive and real. He desires to make you one of His own. If you are ready, you can make this lifetime commitment to follow Jesus. It begins with calling out to Him.

Written below is a prayer for you to say. Something important that you must know, though, is that this prayer shouldn't just be read; it should be meant with all of your heart. You have to mean this when you say it. You are saying this prayer not for me, but for yourself unto God.

Dear God,

I come before You now through Your Son, Jesus Christ. I have sinned against You, but today I choose to believe that Jesus died for me on the cross and rose again three days later. I believe that Jesus is alive and seated at the right hand of Your throne in heaven. I ask for Your forgiveness. Help me to live a life that pleases You as I commit to following You wholeheartedly. Thank You for loving me and never giving up on me. I receive Your forgiveness. Thank You that I am now saved by faith. Thank You for preparing a place for me in heaven. In Jesus' Name, Amen!

If you said this prayer and meant it with all your heart, I want to welcome you to the family of God! Heaven is now celebrating your decision! You now need to get connected with a nearby church, as further discipleship is needed to help you grow as a Christian. I am excited for you! If you're not ready to commit to this prayer, that's okay. I encourage you to read the Bible and find out more about Jesus. May God bless you!

PHOTO ALBUM

**Some of the photos in this album are graphic.
The following album contains images that show
the crash Cody encountered and his injuries.
Viewer discretion is advised.**

Cody performing as a clown at age 6.

Cody juggling fire in the circus.

Cody performing in front of a large group of kids in Cuba.

May 31, 2013
Cody was trapped inside of this burning vehicle.

Picture above shows Cody's hand on the steering wheel.

Cody jammed inside of his vehicle.

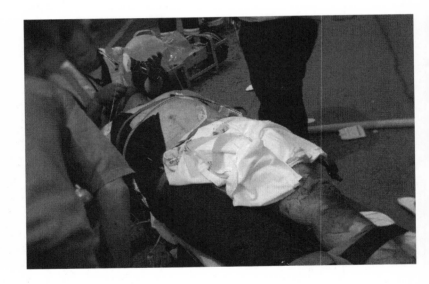

The life flight chopper with Cody inside.

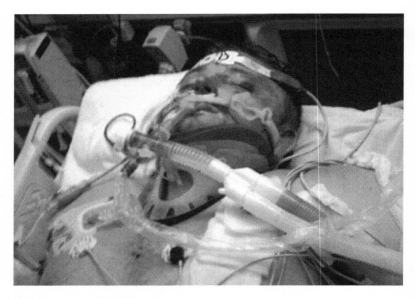

Cody in a coma on full life support.

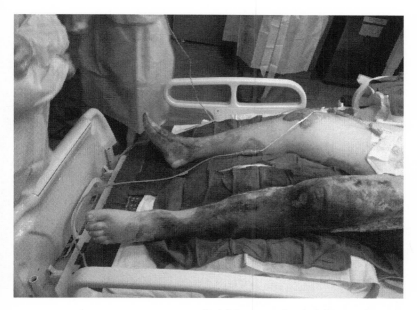

Cody's legs immediately following the crash.

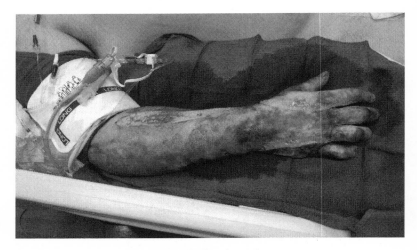

Cody's right arm and hand immediately after the crash.

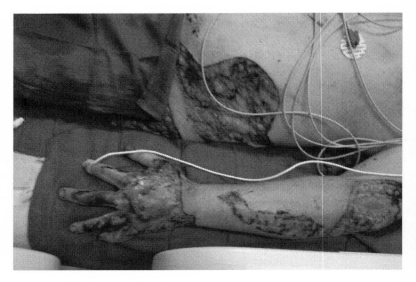

Cody's left side injuries.

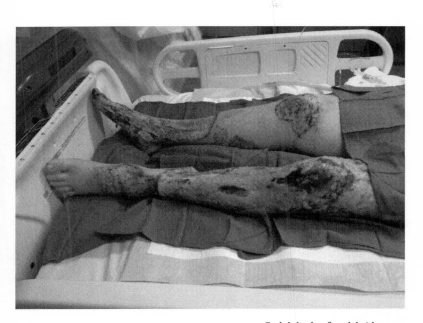

Cody's body after debridement.

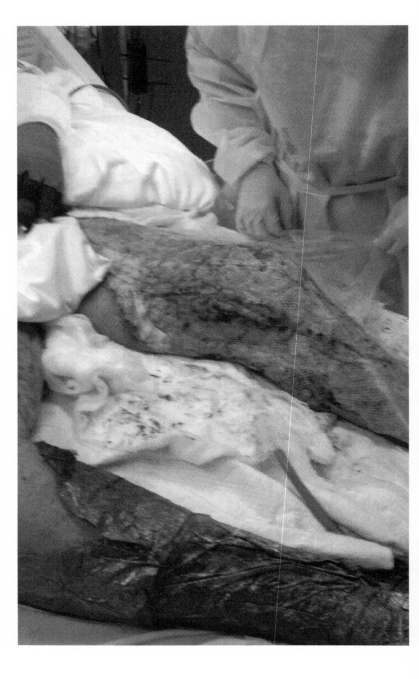

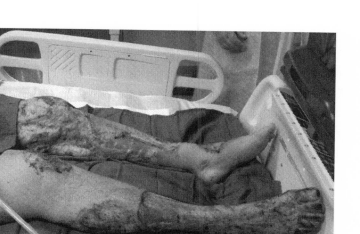

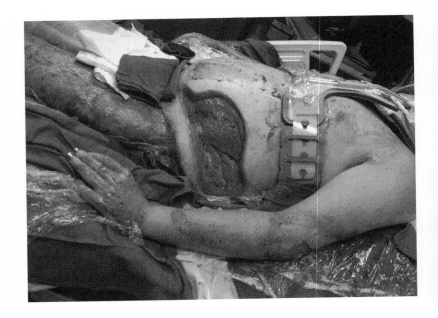

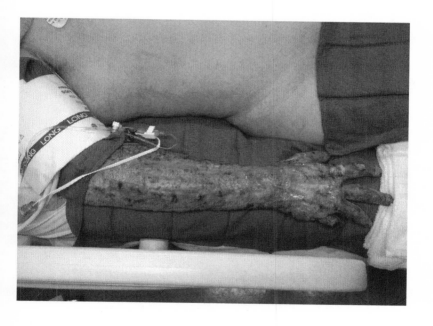

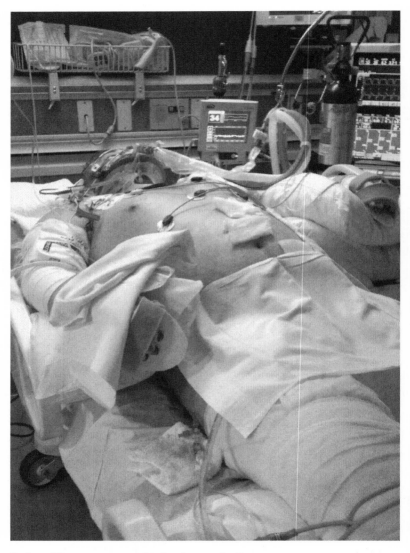

Cody on life support, wrapped in bandages and splints.

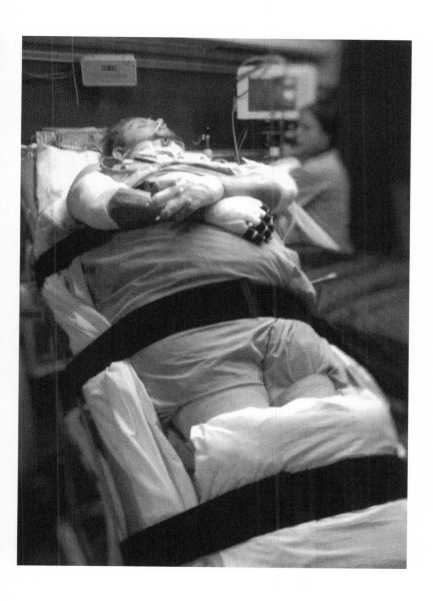

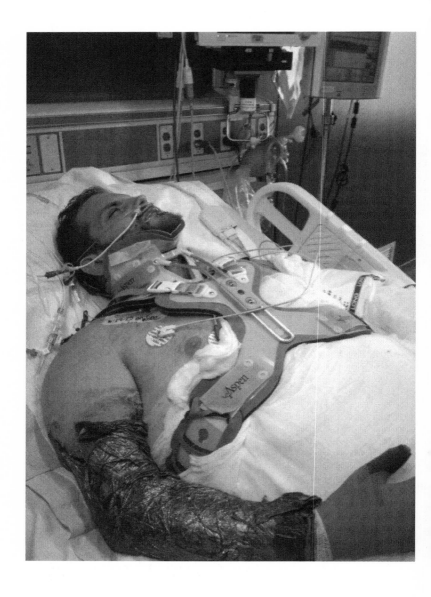

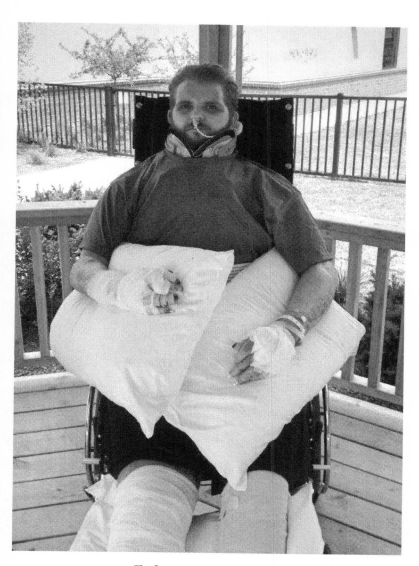

The first time Cody got to go outside while in In-stay rehab.

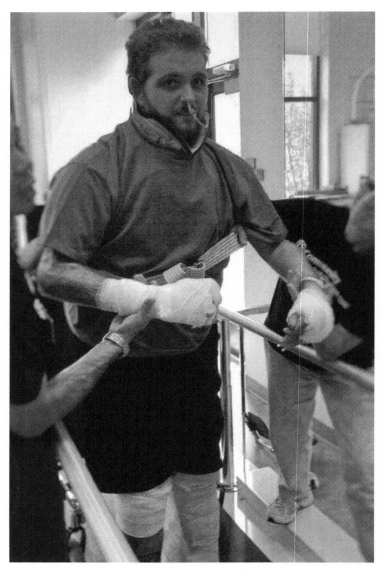

Cody relearning to walk.

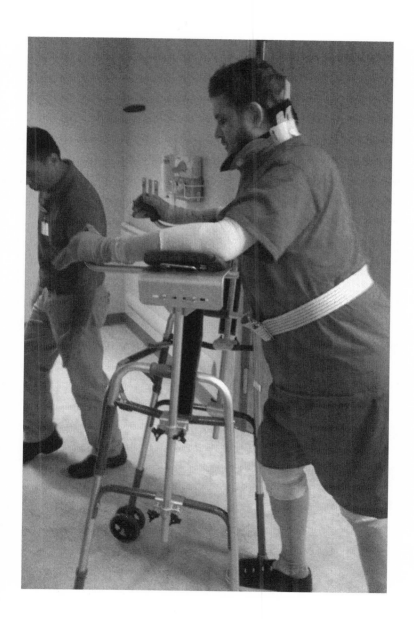

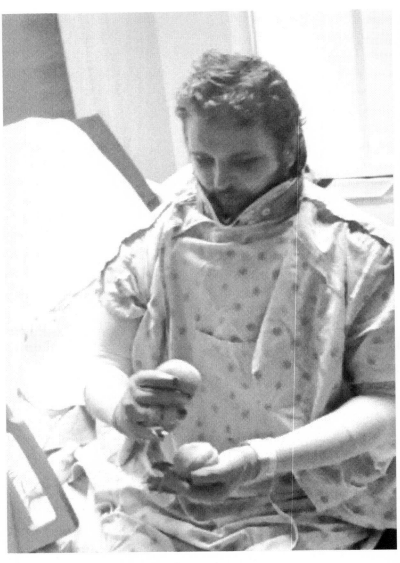

Cody attempting to juggle three beanbags again.

Cody speaking for his hometown months after the crash.

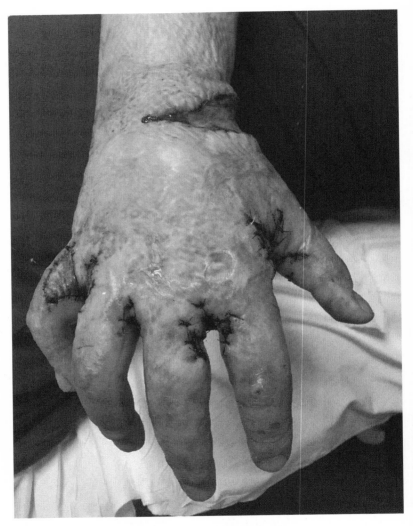

Picture of Cody's right hand following a scar release procedure.

Cody looking at his mangled vehicle a year later.

Cody juggling in the streets of Tampa, FL.

Cody's family.
Mom: Jan Byrns; Dad: Allen Byrns; Brothers: Shane, Jesse, and Toby.

ACKNOWLEDGEMENTS

My Family - for supporting me during the writing of this book.

Sheila - for your encouragement, coaching, and guidance.

Sean - for your coaching and guiding me to be a better speaker.

Shane & Kendall - for your guidance, patience, and editing skills.

Kevin Anderson & Associates - for your editing assistance.

Jeff - for your thoughtful insights and legal guidance.

Ayush - for the wonderful cover design.

Special thanks to the **Gibson County Sheriff's Department** and **The Richard M. Fairbanks Burn Center** for supplying pictures.

And, most importantly, I give all glory and honor to the One who has ordained me to carry His Gospel – **Jesus Christ, my Lord and Savior!**

NOTES

Chapter 2 – Understanding the Scar

1. *Merriam-Webster's Medical Dictionary*. (Springfield, MA: Merriam Webster, Incorporated, 2016), 699.

2. Sood, Rajiv, and Bruce M. Achauer. *Achauer and Sood's Burn Surgery: Reconstruction and Rehabilitation*. (Philadelphia, PA: Saunders Elsevier, 2006), 368.

Chapter 4 – Recognizing Why it Happened

3. "Doesn't Isaiah 45:7 Teach That God Is the Author of Sin?" *Teaching The Word Ministries*, www.teachingtheword.org/apps/ articles/?articleid=59465&blogid=5435.

4. Slick, Matt. "Christian Apologetics & Research Ministry." *b777*. 3 July 2017, carm.org/ does-god-create-evil.

5. "CFNI Lecture with Dave Roever." Daystar Television – Spreading the Gospel by Television & Video, www.daystar.com/ondemand/video/?video=5569088682001.

Chapter 5 – Take Control of the Problem

6. "A Quote by Carol Burnett." *Quote by Carol Burnett: "Only I Can Change My Life. No One Can Do It for..."* www.goodreads.com/quotes/205215-only-i-can-change-my-life-no-one-can-do.

7. "A Quote by Bruce Lee." *Quote by Bruce Lee: "The Successful Warrior Is the Average Man, Wit..."* www.goodreads.com/quotes/461996-the-successful-warrior-is-the-average-man-with-laser-like-focus.

8. "A Quote from The Scar." *Quote by China Miéville: "Scars Are Memory. Like Sutures. They Stitch the..."* www.goodreads.com/quotes/541606-scars-are-memory-like-sutures-they-stitch-the-past-to.

9. Graziosi, Dean. *Millionaire Success Habits: The Gateway to Wealth & Prosperity.* (Phoenix, AZ: Growth Publishing, 2017.) Ch. 2.

Chapter 8 – Embrace Your Story

10. "About Sean Stephenson." *Sean Stephenson.* 4 May 2017. seanstephenson.com/about/.

11. "A Quote by Kaitlyn Walsh." *Quote by Kaitlyn Walsh: "The Key to Success Is Playing the Hand You Were..."* www.goodreads.com/quotes/7031981-the-key-to-success-is-playing-the-hand-you-were.

12. "An Arrow Can Only Be Shot..." *The Quotable Coach.* 2 Sep. 2015. www.thequotablecoach.com/an-arrow-can-only-be-shot/.

Chapter 9 – Live Abundantly

13. "I Still Believe—Dave Roever's Story." I Still Believe—Dave *Roever's Story | Why Is This Happening?* whyisthishappening.org/topics/dave-roever-burned-by-fire.

14. "A Quote by Francis of Assisi." *Quote by Francis of Assisi: "Preach the Gospel at All Times and When Necessa..."* www.goodreads.com/quotes/1475313-preach-the-gospel-at-all-times-and-when-necessary-use.

Subscribe For
Email Newsletters

CodyByrns.com

Giving & Equipping

Learn More At
TheCBFoundation.org

Stay Connected

@TheCodyByrns

Made in the USA
Columbia, SC
02 May 2019